Secrets for
t' Mad

dodie

Secrets for the Mad

OBSESSIONS, CONFESSIONS AND LIFE LESSONS

Keywords PRESS

ATRIA

New York • London • Toronto • Sydney • New Delhi

An Imprint of Simon & Schuster, Inc.
1230 Avenue of the Americas
New York, NY 10020

First Keywords Press/Atria Paperback edition November 2017

Keywords Press/**ATRIA** PAPERBACK and colophons are trademarks of Simon & Schuster, Inc.

For information about special discounts for bulk purchases, please contact Simon & Schuster Special Sales at 1-866-506-1949 or business@simonandschuster.com.

The Simon & Schuster Speakers Bureau can bring authors to your live event. For more information or to book an event, contact the Simon & Schuster Speakers Bureau at 1-866-248-3049 or visit our website at www.simonspeakers.com.

Manufactured in the United States of America

10 9 8 7 6 5 4 3 2 1

Library of Congress Cataloging-in-Publication Data

Names: Clark, Dodie, author.
Title: Secrets for the mad : obsessions, confessions, and life lessons / Dodie Clark.
Description: New York : Atria/Keywords Press, 2017. | Includes bibliographical references and index.
Identifiers: LCCN 2017043514 (print) | LCCN 2017035858 (ebook) | ISBN 9781501180118 (ebook) | ISBN 9781501180101 (paperback)
Subjects: LCSH: Clark, Dodie. | Bloggers—United States—Biography. | Authors, English—21st century—Biography. | BISAC: BIOGRAPHY & AUTOBIOGRAPHY / Personal Memoirs.
Classification: LCC PR6103.L37253 (print) | LCC PR6103.L37253 Z46 2018 (ebook) | DDC 823/.92 [B]—dc23
LC record available at https://lccn.loc.gov/2017043514

ISBN 978-1-5011-8010-1
ISBN 978-1-5011-8011-8 (ebook)

'Hey Sammy, who should I dedicate my book to?'

Sammy's weight falls to one side, his movements suddenly flamboyant. Pouting cheekily, he struts past, hand on hip.

'Me.'

This is for Sammy.

CONTENTS

curtain call

SECRET FOR THE MAD

I've got a secret for the mad;
in a little bit of time it won't hurt so bad.
And I get that I don't get it –
but you will burn right now but then you won't regret it.

You're not gonna believe a word I say,
what's the point in just drowning another day?
And I get that I don't get it –
but the world will show you that you won't regret it.

Little things, all the stereotypes,
they're gonna help you get through this one night,
and there will be a day when you can say you're okay and mean it!

I promise you, it'll all make sense again.

There's nothing to do right now but try;
there are a hundred people who will listen to you cry.
And I get that they don't get it –
but they love you so much that you won't regret it.

You're at the bottom, this is it;
just get through, you will be fixed.
And you think that I don't get it –
but I burned my way through and I don't regret it.

Little things, all the stereotypes,
they're gonna help you get through this one night,
and there will be a day when you can say you're okay and mean it!

I promise you, it'll all make sense again.

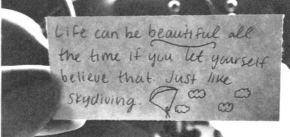

Life can be beautiful all the time if you let yourself believe that. Just like skydiving.

SUNDAY
A1   THE WAILERS
A2   DODIE   SOLD OUT

MORE BIKES LESS CARS

LUNA

'Is she alright?'

It's a sunny spring day in April and my flatmate, Hazel, and I are on our balcony. Jack, Hazel's boyfriend, is making us a cup of tea inside and singing to himself playfully, a light soundtrack of clinks and hums. Below us, about twenty metres away, there's a young girl in her early teens in a black puffa coat sitting on the kerb of the road by a tree and staring off into space. Every now and again the wind blows her hair and she breaks out of her spell, tucking it behind her ear, shuffling her legs and looking around, before settling back into her daze. She's been sitting there for about half an hour while mums push their prams by, barely double taking, their kids running around them like maypole dancers.

Hazel frowns and leans over the balcony.

'She's not, no. She looks like she's . . . getting away a bit.'

I give her a knowing look.

'I've been there.'

'I've been there,' she echoes immediately. We grin at each other and my chest aches as I remember sitting alone on the swings in the park down my road, teeth chattering, head spinning, snot running. Hazel shivers – a similar memory has clearly also just been replayed. We turn back to the girl and sympathetically watch her pick apart her shoes and poke sticks into the ground.

'Should we invite her in? Make her a cup of tea?'

'I'm the one making the tea. What's this?' Jack joins us outside, handing us full hot mugs and collapsing into a garden chair that's facing the sun.

Hazel gestures towards the tree. 'That girl over there. She's not alright.'

Jack leans forward in his chair and peers over the edge.

The girl hugs her chest with folded arms.

'Ah, she's fine. She's probably just waiting for someone.'

Clearly, no chilling memory plays in Jack's head.

* * *

We finish our tea in the sunshine, a happy cycle of side eyes and cackles from Jack as he winds us up, and returned tuts and playful smacks from me and Hazel. They grab their sunglasses and bags and ask if I want to come to town for lunch, but I tell them I want to write today and that I'll join them later for a movie night and spaghetti bolognese round Jack's. We sing our goodbyes, I hear the door close, and then a minute later I hear them shout my nickname from the street.

I peer over the balcony and we make faces and laugh, our shrieks echoing down the road, and then I wave the pair of them off.

I notice the girl glancing up, watching our dumb games and staring as Jack and Hazel turn the corner. She looks up at me. I smile back and quickly look to my laptop. I type a line that I've already written, suddenly embarrassed that I'm being watched, and eager to give off the impression that I am working.

For the next ten minutes we have an unspoken awareness and curiosity of each other.

Out of the corner of my eye I see her stand up and walk away from the tree, towards me. I close my laptop, stand up and rest my arms on the railing.

'Are you alright?'

'I'm not, no.'

I grab my keys, shove on my ballet slippers and rush out the door.

* * *

Her name is Luna. She's fourteen, she suffers from anxiety, and her parents don't understand. She lives about an hour away and she's told them she's off to see her schoolfriends and that she'll be back by four. She got on a train and somehow ended up here, sat by a tree and then saw us laughing on our balcony. She stayed in sight, secretly hoping we'd notice her and come down to chat. Which she seems to feel a lot of shame about.

We slowly walk side by side, and she pours out her worries and insecurities. When she does her hair in the morning, she obsesses over how everyone will look at it in the day. She plays over sentences she messed up months ago, convinced it still brings as much embarrassment to the people around her as it does to her now. She feels lazy and worried that she'll never get into university because she can't finish her homework on time.

This girl is scared of everything.

'My mum booked me an appointment with the doctor because my chest hurt so much. They couldn't find anything wrong with the stethoscope, so they asked me how school was. And I told them it was terrible. And that's how I found out I have anxiety,' she babbles, scuffing stones on the pavement as we amble down the street. 'I took an autism test and I'm apparently on the Asperger spectrum too. Which I didn't really understand at first? And then I read how you might not like parties and how social things scare you and I was like, oh, yeah, that makes sense.'

We walk to the park and get ice creams with strawberry sauce on top. She's terrified of everything. I wonder how someone so talkative could ever be as quiet as she says she is; until I realise I'm a stranger, and she's pouring out years of built-up fear.

We talk about family, friends and then crushes. 'Actually, I'm going out with this boy accidentally, kinda because he's this pop punk singer's godson. He said he liked me and then the whole band showed up at our school? So I said I liked him back, when I don't actually know if I do. I know, it's really bad. I'm the worst.'

I smirk, jumping back into teenage-me brain and remembering the cringe-filled months of dating someone I didn't fancy because someone liked me.

'It's alright, I'm not judging. That's what being a teenager is for – you make mistakes, things get shitty, and then you learn from them.'

'Things get shitty?' She turns to me, and it's as if I can feel her heart rate increase. I frown.

I revisit teenage-me for a moment. Suddenly I'm seeing everything through her eyes, and my chest closes up. My brain is a chaotic mess; the world is vivid, exciting, terrifying. School is overwhelming, my family is draining, and the future is unbearable; everything is a question, and I hate myself. I step out of her eyes, back into the brain of my twenties, and breathe a sigh of relief. I smile, and I know what to say.

'I had a granny when I was your age, whom I loved more than anything in the world. She'd meet me outside school with sweets and magazines, and rub my cold hands together in the winter to warm them up. I knew that she was old, and I knew one day she would die, and I knew that on that day, the world would end. I couldn't fathom the amount of pain losing someone like her would bring. She couldn't die; I wouldn't be able to handle it.'

Luna turns white.

'Well, she died. Of course. And guess what? The world didn't end.'

'It was horrible. You know, the funeral was literally the worst day of my life, my mum got sick from grief, and it hurt, so, much. It hurt a lot for a long time. And I still miss her now, sometimes. But years went by, it wasn't terrible every second, and it got easier every day. Now it's just something that happened, and we all laugh and smile and we can talk about her and it doesn't hurt so much anymore.

'Me and my family all lived in one house, and it was always going to be that way. Like, logically, I knew that I'd move out? But even if that happened I'd still have my little room, and mum and dad would always live in a messy, dark, homey shithole in Epping, arguing every day over who forgot to buy milk. There was no way that could ever change, because if it did the world would end and I wouldn't know who I am any more. Can you see where this is heading?'

Luna stares at me intently. She nods.

'So yeah, when I'm seventeen, I learn that one day my family will blow up. I won't go into logistics but essentially I find out a secret that I keep for four years, blah blah blah, it's all very traumatic, and last year it comes out and everything goes apeshit. I spend a year parenting my parents, our family house gets sold, and there are strangers in my little room, measuring the wardrobes I kept my toys in and discussing where the desk is going to go in Iain's room. It's horrible, it's sad. We drive around the corner of the road I used to ride my bike down, and I say goodbye and ugly cry so loud it feels like my throat is about to explode. But the world doesn't end. Yes, it's painful, and I'm confused about my new identity of someone whose parents are split up, and yes, it's an ongoing weird battlefield of a family. But we all still love each other in our weird way, and it's taught me so much about myself that I'd never have known. In fact, the idea of everyone still living in that house now seems ridiculous. I'd never go back.'

I swallow, my throat tightening.

'I had a best friend called Alice. She lived across the road from me, and we used to open our windows and have conversations across the street. No one will ever know me as well as Alice used to know me, and I'll never be as comfortable around another human as I was with her. Every day with her was filled with uncontrollable laughter and indescribable happiness; we had hundreds of private jokes that could trigger fits of giggles at any point in the day, and we'd write several-page letters of how much we loved each other and how proud we were to know one another. We'd have sleepovers every week and we'd sit in our facemasks, chewing Haribo and vowing to get married at thirty if we hadn't found love. We dreamed of us rocking in our chairs with silver hair in the final years of our lives, still quoting our dumb phrases that we crafted as teens. The day I found it difficult or awkward to talk to Alice would be the day the world would end, because then I'd be alone, and no one would ever love me or know me that much again.

'I went out with a jealous boy who I moved hundreds of miles away for, and Alice went to university in a different place. We talked less and less and then not at all, for about a year. I guess I relied on the idea that when we'd see each other the time and distance apart wouldn't matter? Because we were Alice and Dodie, and that would never change. But it did change – we changed. On different sides of the country. So when we met up again, for the first time, it was difficult. And awkward.

'I'll admit – the world did end a little bit for this one. Especially because on her wall in her uni bedroom there were pages of letters from someone else containing private jokes that I didn't know about. I brought my facemask packs and Haribo sweets and they stayed in my bag because it felt too weird to ask, and we'd both forgotten how to talk to each other.

'If teenage me had known that this would have happened she definitely wouldn't have wanted to live through it. She'd have crawled into a little hole and given up on everything completely. But thankfully I didn't know, so I had to trek through it all; and now it's okay. We had a little break, where we both grew up, and it was unbearable for a bit. But now when I talk to Alice there's no tiptoeing around, or burning jealousy, and it's almost back to how we used to talk, except we've both grown up a little.

'Someone wonderful in my music class got cancer and died. I took a gap year after school ended because I was so confused and terrified I couldn't handle writing a personal statement. I didn't revise as well as I could have done in year thirteen and ended up with not the best grades. I was so scared of getting depression, and guess what? I have a lovely little cocktail of mental health problems. I was terrified of all these things, and they all happened. And things got shitty.'

Luna's brow furrows. I should probably evaluate quickly.

'My point is, a lot of my worst fears came true; fears that felt so big I could barely hold them in my brain. Things are going to get weird and bad in your life, and your brain demands that you prepare for them as best as you can; when, really, there's not much point in worrying about them before because you never know when or how they will happen, and actually they're never really as bad as you think they will be. The world doesn't end. In fact, it pushes on and demands to keep spinning through all sorts of mayhem, and you survive through. And because you survive through, you learn lessons about how to be a stronger, kinder, better human – lessons you can only learn by going through these sorts of things.'

We stop walking, and I turn to her, smiling. I am digging through years of pain, things that I never thought I could talk about to anyone, let alone a stranger – but it's alright. I've never realised how proud of myself I am.

'All of my shit that happened? I wouldn't have wanted it any other way, because I'm so grateful for how each experience has shaped me.

I've learned to love myself through them, and while I'm not saying it's easy to be excited about possiblde disasters, I just want to say that whatever happens – you can and will be okay. More than okay.'

Luna nibbles the skin around her thumbnail for a bit. We start walking again, both licking the drips running down our cones. I slurp up the remaining ice cream and crunch into the waffle, while Luna chucks hers in a bin we pass by.

'What?! You throw away the cone? That's the best bit! What's wrong with you!' I say playfully.

'A lot, obviously. That's what I've been trying to tell you,' she jokes back.

On the way back to my flat, I learn that Luna's good at guitar, and that she's in a band she named 'Einstein's Monsters' after her favourite book of short stories. She's also very witty and funnier than I'll ever be, although most of her one-liners are self-deprecating. I listen to her babble and casually use her self-doubt to make us laugh, and I suddenly realise how stupid and illogical insecurity is. It is unfair that wonderful people have to work so hard to get to a place where they can understand that they are wonderful.

* * *

We reach my door and stop to squint and smile at each other in the sunshine.

'Well, I should probably get back home. And you should probably keep going with your writing.' Luna shuffles.

I suddenly raise my brows in response to a little spark in my head. 'Can I write about you?'

Luna sticks out her bottom lip. 'Why?'

'Because you're so inspiring.'

Luna looks down, hiding a flushed smile.

'I'd have to change your name though. What would you like to be called?'

She looks up, grinning. 'Einstein's Monster?'

I laugh.

She looks around. 'Um . . . Luna? That's the name of my cat.'

I like it.

We hug, thank each other and wave goodbye, and I hop up the stairs, close the door, grab my laptop, and immediately start typing.

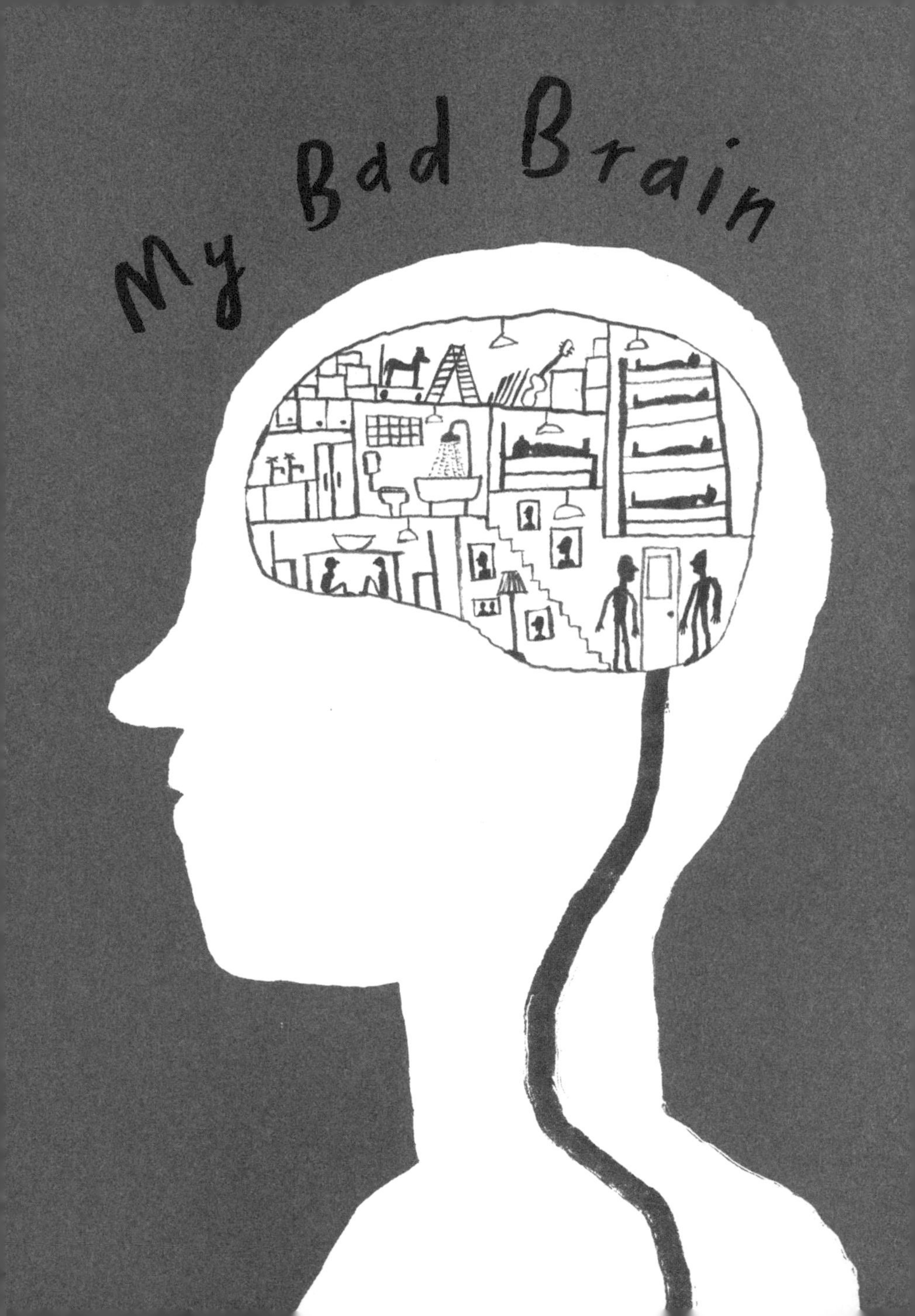
My Bad Brain

DOWN

I woke up as heavy as lead,
an ocean of worry weighs me down in bed.

But there's things to do!
There's a life to live;
must ignore my stupid head.

Friends float above in the wind,
bright balloons pulling them up as they grin.

But there's things to do!
There's a life to live;
must ignore the things I think.

It's like walking around with a stone for a heart,
people swimming in honey as your life falls apart.
It's cold and it's dark
and there's no way out.
'I felt like you once!'
I wish I could shout.

You can never undo the brain;
now it knows of the holes it will fall as it's trained.

Cause there's things to do,
there's a life to live;
watch them laugh while you stay in the rain.

FIREWORKS

My chest and armpits are hot and itchy under the several layers of thermals and jumpers Mum has yanked over my head. Walking stiffly upstairs, I waddle to my bedroom, rip off my gloves and grab my jelly baby money box. It rattles and I excitedly pull a £10 note from the bottom, crumpling it in my hand. A squeak bubbles up from my stomach as I imagine the bright lights, the smell of smoke in cold air, the glow sticks I will buy and keep in my room to play with at bedtime for days after.

As Mum and Dad talk in the front of the car, I stare out the window at the orange lights in the black night and my brain explodes with vivid imaginations. Smiling in front of thousands of people, applauding me on a giant stage. Flying around my school, my teachers looking up, baffled, but with gasps of admiration and awe. Time stopping, allowing me to walk up to my bullies and step on their toes and draw on their faces and tell them they're ugly. Being stranded on an island, with a tiger as my best friend who allows me to ride on his back, my hands sinking into his bright, rough fur. My stomach jumps around and my heart aches at the worlds I build. I mime to music that isn't playing and manage to squeeze a tear out of my eye for my imaginary music video.

It smells like wet grass, burning wood and fried onions. I hear screams of joy from spinning funfair rides and my mum tickles my wrist with her little finger from the hand I'm holding.

I giggle and pull away, looking up at her.

'Mummy, can I go on the chair planes?'

'Mummy, can I have some candyfloss?'

'Mummy, can I have that rainbow wand?'

'Please? Please? Please?'

My cheeks are full of white bread and ketchup, and then hot chocolate and cakey waffles, and then sharp vinegar-soaked mushy chips. I stare up into the sky and coo at the pink, gold and green sparks in the black.

* * *

From my closed eyes and loose body position, I feel the car reverse and sink familiarly. It is quiet and I try not to crack a smile as I hear my parents turn back and feel their eyes on me.

My dad scoops me up into his arms and carries me into the house. I don't break character as he gently places me into my bed. He slots Andy Pandy into my arms and kisses me on my cheek.

The light switch is flicked off and the door is closed. I wait a few more seconds, pull the wand I bought out of my pocket, and stare into the flashing lights, making shadow friends on my ceiling, inviting them into my duvet cave and chatting to them about the magic powers I was born with.

SEVEN-YEAR-OLD DODIE'S HOPES FOR THE FUTURE

I will never grow up. I'm not like everyone else – I am special! And I know that older-me will agree too. We will always choose to have fun – adults will sunbathe and we will splash in the pool and pretend to be mermaids. Adults will wear brown suits and eat mushrooms and we will slurp spaghetti hoops for breakfast in our tutus. Adults will worry about everything but we will eat cake if we feel sad and have pillow fort parties to feel better.

I will be like the nice lady in the pink dress on the telly who reads stories and sings to the puppets in the rainbow world, or I will be like Miss Watkins and be a teacher but let everyone know in my class that I'm secretly just a kid like them, and then give everyone extra playtime. I would like to be a ballerina, but Daddy says that all they eat is salad and, although I love salad, I really do like pizza and chicken nuggets too.

One day I won't go to school and I won't live with Mum and Daddy but that is so far away I don't really believe it'll ever happen. Granny says that she will go to heaven one day and it makes me scared, but that also feels so far away, like it will never happen, so I don't think or worry about it too much. I hope when these things do happen and I am scared and sad I will just go to the park and go on the swings because that will always make me feel happy. I am a happy person and I will always be able to cheer myself up and everyone around me with my smile!

I hope that someone will teach me how to do everything in the world. I don't know how to ride a bus or how banks work and it all seems very big and difficult, like when Daddy talks about space and the universe and science. One day I will be as clever as him and he will be so proud of me. I like it when Daddy says he is proud of me.

I've got so much I want to think about
I feel weird. Am I depressed?
Sometimes I think I am. Right now
I do. Other times I think I'm getting
better.

THE THEME PARK'S
STOPPED WORKING

If I had to describe my brain before I started experiencing darkness, I would say it was deep thinking, excited, but most of all, it was BUSY. If you were to dive into my brain at seven years old, you'd be plunged into vivid imaginations of magical fantasies; colossal, complex worlds of made-up characters and storylines, where in each one I was, of course, the star. Throughout teenagehood I still visited these worlds, but introduced my crushes and celebrity friends, passionate kisses and dramatic situations reaching their peak of extravagance. There were cogs in my brain that were rapidly spinning; the insides of my head constantly whirring and clicking; a theme park in my mind bursting with exhilaration, anxiety, fire, euphoria.

* * *

When I was in my last years of school, three things happened.

* My granny passed away, and I experienced true grief for the first time in my life. I watched my mum shrink and fall into depression.

* I started loving a boy, and realised too late that he liked to shout at me. (As I was in a relationship, I went on hormonal-altering contraception.)

* In a coffee shop in London, I was given a monstrously heavy secret. My brain couldn't comprehend or process the information, so it flipped upside down. (This isn't something I'm in a place to talk about right now – maybe ever – but know it was significant enough to have a huge impact on my life.)

I spent a while walking around confused. My theme park brain was running messily; carts rolling off their tracks, fireworks exploding too early in the sky, fantasies interrupted by aggressive men and their wolf eyes. I held my boyfriend's hand, walking through London Underground and wondering who turned up the brightness in my eyes and why I was so sleepy all the time. I asked him if I was dreaming. He said I'd wake up soon, but I never did.

I moved to a different city when I was eighteen; an experiment of adulthood, and a wonder that if I started a new purpose then all of this confusion would go away. I packed up bits of my little room into cardboard boxes, took them 120 miles away from my home, and dotted them around a cold, echoey house up a hill. My head had still been spinning up until this point, but slowing, dulling, until eventually, in the early hours of the morning, while lying teary-eyed and scared next to my sleeping boyfriend, my theme park brain just . . . stopped.

My emotions sank through the holes in my mind, any sort of passion or feeling whatsoever disappearing down the drain. The final flicker dimmed and then snuffed; a sliver of smoke the only reminder of the vigorous fire that once was. Everything was replaced with one thing: a vacuous, hollowing, overwhelming feeling of despair.

I was a shell of a normal girl; the drama classes I'd taken as a child finally paying off as I managed to convince the world that I still had a soul. After a few months of empty smiles and dark headaches, I asked my mum to book me an appointment at the doctor's.

'What can I help you with today?' A rosy-faced woman beamed at me in her cushioned chair.

I pulled out my phone, trembling, and shakily read her the paragraph I'd typed up in the waiting room. I stumbled over how I'd run home to fall asleep as quickly as possible, just so I could shut down and not have to think any more. How I'd wake up at 3 a.m., nauseous from the nightmares that felt like black holes inside my being. I skipped over the scars on my thighs from the nights I dragged the edge of scissors along my skin, relishing the distraction of surface-level pain and coming the closest to feeling something I'd had in ages.

She looked down with a slight smile while I mumbled through.

'Are you studying, Dorothy?' she asked as I finished. I plastered on my usual polite smile and told her about my move to Bath, my YouTube channel, and the hopes for the future I'd planned when my brain was working. She wowed and cooed, asking questions about my travels while my throat closed up and my heart sank as I realised I was being patronised.

'I don't think you are depressed. It's very dangerous to give someone so young a label like that. You're doing so many activities, travelling around the world, making new friends – it's certainly more than I did at your age!'

I felt the back of my neck get hot and tears sting my eyes. I wanted to shout, what's the point when I didn't really experience or enjoy any of it?!

But I nodded and stretched my smile, whispering a 'thank you' and grabbing my coat to walk out before I started crying. I wasn't going to be listened to or believed, and I couldn't stand the room any longer. It took three years until I built up the courage to go back to the doctors to talk about my mental health.

* * *

Since then, I've learned much more about my darkness. I broke up with my angry boyfriend, came off the hormonal altering contraception I'd been on, and welcomed back the first emotions I'd felt in about a year. I ran around in the sunshine and started to remember what hope felt like. I certainly wasn't cured – every now and again I'd find myself swallowed up into the void of nothingness and I'd spend months at a time forgetting how to live. The waves of depression taught me that there's always an up after a down, and that my bad brain sneers and tells convincing lies about fighting it being pointless.

With every new experience, good or bad, I'd shared what I had learned from it online through music and other forms of art, opening up to thousands, and then hundreds of thousands, and then millions of people who can relate in different ways. I use my voice to spread awareness of troublesome minds, and to create communities for people who are also struggling to feel grounded.

There's only so much you can say in songs, poems, even videos. You let the feelings overwhelm you and then you find neat little phrases to sum them up. Other people will find them and fill their own meaning in the gaps, and sometimes it matches with yours, but sometimes what you truly wanted to say will be missed by some people. And obviously that's okay, that's what art is for – but I wanted a place to share the depths behind the music and let the world in to my turbulent mind. The last thing I want in the world is to create any more drama for myself (which is a ridiculous thing to hold on to when you open yourself up as much as you can to millions of strangers who can judge you anonymously, especially when there are still large chunks of information and back story missing that you have to keep for the safety of yourself and for other people). I don't share for gossip, or for attention; I write, create and share to offload some of the weight from my mind by turning it into something useful and good. I want to share the stories of the ways I lost my young theme park brain, for those who also feel as though the funfair lights are flickering, and for those who cannot understand how it could ever stop working.

I have learned so much from my pain, and from sharing and connecting with others, and finding the good in my 'madness'. I am far from better (in fact, I'm not in the best headspace while writing this book), but I am absolutely hopeful. I miss my young brain so, so much, but oddly enough, I would never trade it in for my experienced, slightly damaged one now. The theme park in my mind shrank into a little corner, and although I can't visit it any more, I can still just about see a small girl flying around her colourful world, holding hands with her idols and saving people with her magical powers – the happy hero of many stories.

I wish I remember how to cry

I think my brain will never go back to normal
I think I just have to like my life with
this new confused, forever unhappy state
of mind

A brain that is CONSTANTLY waiting to be
fixed, and for life to begin

WHEN

I think I've been telling lies,
cause I've never been in love.
Everyone falls for the sunshine disguise,
distracted by who they're thinking of.

I'd rather date an idea –
something I'll never find.
Sure, I'll live in the moment,
but I'm never happy here;
I'm surrounded by greener looking time.

Am I the only one
wishing life away?
Never caught up in the moment,
busy begging the past to stay.
Memories painted with much brighter ink;
they tell me I loved, teach me how to think.

I'll take what I can get
cause I'm too damp for a spark.
Kissing sickly sweet guys
cause they say they like my eyes,
but I'd only ever see them in the dark.

I'm sick of faking diary entries,
got to get it in my head – I'll never be sixteen again.
I'm waiting to live, and waiting to love,
oh, it'll be over, and I'll still be asking when.

Am I the only on
wishing life away?
Never caught up in the moment,
busy begging the past to stay.
Memories painted with much brighter ink;
they tell me I loved, teach me how to think.

I'm sick of faking diary entries,
got to get it in my head – I'll never be sixteen again.
I'm waiting to live, still waiting to love,
oh, it'll be over, and I'll still be asking when,
oh, it'll be over, and I'll still be asking when.

Sat 11 Oct 2014

I don't understand what's wrong with my brain?

I just don't... think... anymore.

Do you even want to cry anymore?
Not particularly

What does remembering feel like? what
does emotion feel like? or memories?

What does it feel like to be alive?
Because I've fucking forgot.

Just flipped back to the first few pages.
I miss feeling.

I don't fucking understand me anymore

I JUST CAN'T REMEMBER
ANYTHING.

I'm not taking anything in.
Summer happened... I guess
it's winter now
Where is my brain –

WHY CAN'T I CRY

'HELLO THERE, YES, I'M JUST CALL-ING ABOUT MY WORSENING MEN-TAL STATE?'

I have a slight suspicion that I've actually been sleeping and dreaming through my days since I was about eighteen. The timeline of my life seems to have a massive wall straight down the middle – a distinct before and after of feeling spaced out. Up until last year I knew that something was definitely different, but I'd never heard of anyone who felt the same. I'd travel and watch my friends absorb a beautiful view of the night sky, or the sea stretched out for miles in front, and I'd rub my eyes, opening and closing and widening them in an attempt for them to work how they used to and allow me to see the world in full.

In 2015 I travelled around Australia and New Zealand twice, LA and Florida, and also around the UK multiple times on tour – and I can't really remember any of it. Memories of my childhood and school life are clear, vibrant; I watch back moments where I'd drink in a situation, fully marking that present time as beautiful; gazing and adoring my life. I could have told you about the movie I saw a week ago and all my favourite bits, and recounted the conversation in the Pizza Hut, a vivid chunk stored neatly in my head. Now, in this present moment, I'm trying to remember where I was yesterday, and all I'm getting is 'file not found'. There is nothing more frustrating than reaching for a memory and grabbing empty handfuls of air. If I do have memories, they are played on a tiny, slightly warped screen, a small, fuzzy snapshot of time at the back of my head, its place of order in a timeline unknown.

When I was younger, I used a pocket camcorder to film my adventures so I could watch back my day in bed and relive the joy. Now I document as much as I can to desperately hold on to the memories of my early adulthood. When I recount stories of the roadtripping I apparently did through California, or the ziplining in Auckland, I steal smiles and phrases from the footage I took of 'myself' when I was there. It is so strange to watch a girl laugh and seemingly enjoy the scenes around her, but know that behind those eyes is my dark, obsessive, cloudy mind.

But, like I said, there was no name for what I was experiencing (or rather wasn't experiencing). I attributed it to growing up, guessing adulthood just lacked the clarity of youth. I slapped my cheeks and pinched my arms in an attempt to 'wake up' in social situations. I even got my eyes tested, convinced that I had some sort of a loss of vision which was restricting me from seeing anything properly. When I was coming out of my two-year depression, after my relationship ended that year, I felt hopeful and glowed about how much better I felt emotionally – but I knew that something big was still missing.

* * *

In the spring of 2016, my stress levels were peaking as I took on far too much work and travel. I'd been working as a presenter for an online channel, and we were to travel to Wales for a high-energy three-day shoot, so I pushed down the warning signs from my body and trekked on. Over those days I noticed that my vision was getting so bad it was like I could only see whatever pinpoint thing I was looking at – the complete rest of my peripheral vision was silver, like TV static. I was so tired my eyes felt itchy and heavy, my head aching as if I was hungover. It did feel like I was drunk, or on something; whenever I talked my words hung in the air in front of me, as if it were a recording. My own voice didn't belong to me and yet it sounded so scarily familiar. I was terrified I'd accidentally been spiked . . . I guess by something that stayed in your system for a long period of time? So I'd go to bed early, desperate to wake up feeling okay, or okay as I was before. But I'd open my eyes, unsure if I was in a dream, and get out of bed, frowning and touching the walls to confirm that I was actually awake.

I somehow got through the shoot, desperate to get home to my flat in London, hopeful that the return to familiarity would fix whatever this was. I lugged my suitcase up the stairs, put my key in the door, walked in to my living room and saw a stranger lying on my sofa.

'Alright, babe? How was Wales?'

I couldn't compute Hazel's face in my head. My flat looked humongous and tiny at the same time. I struggled to reply in the same way I would if I were hammered and was trying to act sober.

'Hazel, I've gone mad.'

* * *

I called every helpline I could find. I remained calm and rational, somehow still putting on my 'phone voice' when talking about an extremely personal situation. It was probably quite a comical juxtaposition; a girl with a tear-streamed face and snot running down her nose hyperventilating to hold music, composing herself just in time with a clear spoken 'Hello there, yes, I'm just calling about my worsening mental state?'

For some reason I couldn't get the help I really needed. I was sure I needed more than just someone to talk to – so the Samaritans weren't much help. The medical numbers I called asked me if I was signed up to a GP – which I wasn't – and then told me if it was an emergency, and if I was suicidal, I should hang up and call 999.

The word 'suicidal' to me had always meant something different to what I now know it to be. I thought that people who were suicidal wanted to die, and that they weren't scared of it.

I didn't want to die, I very much wanted to live. That's all I wanted, and I was desperate to find out how to do that again, because I wasn't; and that was the problem. I felt like I was in this weird limbo where I was technically 'alive', but not getting anything from existing but pain, and I knew that if that's all life was from now on I couldn't possibly do it any more. Death was still absolutely terrifying and far too big to think about; so my head would dodge around the actual concept of somehow performing the action and suppress it with the idea that it was the best option. In between hopeless calls, it would poke its ginormous head around the corner, arrogant and overbearing, like Truth: the one solution that had a definite outcome of relief.

Nevertheless I kept trying. I'd dug through the bin bags Hazel had placed outside to try to find a proof of address for me to use to sign up to the doctor's down the road. I'd found an old, ketchup-stained gas bill from the beginning of the year, walked briskly with it clutched in my hand, my passport and keys in the other, and opened the door, telling my body to talk and move in the way humans do.

'Hello, I'd like to sign up to this practice, please.'

The receptionist swivelled on her chair and grabbed a pen and two pieces of paper from a drawer.

'You'll need to fill these in, and bring them up with a proof of address and some form of identification.'

'Thanks.' I tried my best to give a polite smile, my heart racing. 'Oh, I couldn't find a very recent bill. Will this one be alright?'

She unfolded the crumpled paper from my hand and stared at it blankly, chewing on her gum.

'Yeah, this is from January?' – as if I didn't know – 'You'll need to bring one that's from the last three months. Thank you.' She looked behind me at the next person. I stepped to the side, my throat closing up. I tried to say a pathetic 'please', but nothing would come out. So, of course, I bolted out the door before I started sobbing in front of everyone.

* * *

I sat alone in my flat, wondering if there was a way to detach my brain from my body so I could go on a walk and get a break from the spiralling. I knew that I was sinking deeper and deeper, but unfortunately my rotting brain was very much stuck to my neck and shoulders, and so I stayed in the same spot for hours, snot and tears pouring out while I filled my room with loud, ugly crying. If you've ever been alone and let yourself cry as much as you need to without judgement, you will know how horrific and guttural crying as an adult can sound. The many friends who knew about my darkness and had made me promise to 'call at any time if I ever needed someone to just spill out to' sat in my phonebook, smiling ignorantly at me. The idea of trying to explain what was going on to any of these people was ridiculous; my pain had made me bitter, and I didn't want any patronising 'do you need me to come over? I'm dropping everything and coming over NOW (because I am a GOOD friend)' or 'I understand, we've all been there' sorts of phrases. What I was going through was absolutely incomparable, and I couldn't stand the thought of anyone telling me 'it was going to be okay' because they just had no fucking idea.

I cancelled all my plans for the next few days and ended up going home to Epping. I was still clinging on to the idea that familiarity would help; I suppose when I said I wanted to go home, I think I meant the period of time rather than the place. Mam did her best to look after me – layering me in blankets and making me tea after tea. She placed her hands on my body and tried to will away the pain, like she used to do in my childhood days of stomach migraines; except I wasn't a little girl with a poor tummy, I was a woman in her twenties who had completely forgotten who she was and how to exist with black holes in her head. And my bedroom wasn't my little room with arts and crafts club dreamcatchers and pink curtains, it was brown and full of boxes, envelopes and the shell of the human who once lived and loved.

The next few days were weird. I visited my old primary school with my sister Hedy ('visited' is the wrong word; we broke in to the playground, as the grounds had been shut down for years). We wandered around the incredibly familiar place that seemed to have sprouted foliage and rotted wood in seconds, and I showed her the hopscotch where I fell and scraped my knee in year four; the tree where Amelia Martin had dared me to swear; the wall Jessica Monikendom and I had performed handstands against at break time. We sat in the middle of the playground and I cried, angry and upset that I couldn't find the happy me who ran around in a summer dress in the same spot a decade ago. I travelled back to London and did a lot of walking around, staring at smiling people in parks and wondering how they weren't mad like me. I had no idea where to go or what to do or how to live – I had completely lost myself, and I was terrified I'd never find her again.

I can't remember the order of the ways that I found myself again, but there were three distinct pillars that grounded me and gave me enough hope to claw my way back.

I went through my contacts, searching for someone who might understand so I didn't have to waste time explaining how bad it was. I messaged my friend Tom, who I knew battled severe depression.

'Are you busy?' It looked so pathetic.

It took less than ten seconds for Tom to reply.

'Wanna call?'

I guess my message had a familiar tone.

I video called, neither of us giving a crap about my crumpled blotchy forehead or the amount of slime coming out my nostrils. It was unbelievably relieving to talk to someone who understood so deeply. We even laughed about the lunacy of the situation.

My friend Steven came over. He listened while I cried. Then Hazel came home. Hazel is usually one to give tough love; you come to her with a problem and she'll immediately tell you straight, blunt advice – incredible for heartbreak, where logic can combat emotion, but useless where there can be no logic, like a spiralling brain. She recognised this, and instead gave me company and compassion, sitting me on the sofa, giving me a glass of wine (though I didn't drink it), placing a cushion in my arms and sitting across with Steven, listening and nodding to my wails.

My rotting brain had lied to me; of course talking would help. Of course my loving, caring friends telling me it would get better would help. They fed ropes down the hole I'd been digging, and even if they couldn't pull me up, they at least reminded me that there was a world beyond this, where I'd been before.

Steven hugged me goodbye, leaving me with the same 'I am here whenever you need me' promise he had made before; except this time I accepted it, and logged it in my head as a lifeline for when I next sat in my room, stuck with my thoughts. Hazel wished me goodnight and left her door cracked open, an invitation for company at any point in the night. I sat cross-legged on my carpet, distracting myself online while scratching up and down my legs softly and looking around my room every now and again, still aching and desperately trying to hold on to my existence. As I scrolled up and down the page, a face that caught my attention flashed on my screen. I scrolled back to find a thumbnail of a video Tessa and I had filmed a few weeks before that I had completely forgotten about. In my struggling state I had taken a few days off from the internet, and so had missed the memo that this would have been uploaded today – so I curiously clicked, took a deep breath and leaned closer to my laptop.

And there she was.

I watched her laugh. I watched her dance around a hotel room with someone she loves, I watched her sing and smile and play and express emotion, and I knew that I was looking into a face of genuine happiness. This girl had put on make-up in a hotel bathroom and had grinned at her reflection; not to make sure that it was really her she was looking at, simply pleased about her choice of T-shirt and excited to make music with her friend. They had finished writing a song together, both brains spinning healthily, ideas and talent woven together to create something fun and beautiful. This happy girl in the screen was wearing a pinafore dress that lay crumpled in a corner of my room, hanging out of a suitcase the same functioning girl had packed before. There was evidence of her everywhere: she had stuck pink Post-it notes up on her walls as reminders of the tasks she would complete; her wardrobes were full of spontaneously bought scarves, cardigans and flower crowns thanks to encouraging pals on sunny shopping trips; there was a keyboard, a guitar, two ukuleles, all of which had been sung along with and written feelings-heavy songs on. There were endless signs that the happy, human girl in that video lived in this room and had enjoyed a functioning, joyful life.

I paused the video and looked in the mirror. I saw dark eyes that sat in a pale face, a straight mouth and a tangle of brown hair.

I stretched my lips up, and she smiled at me.

She almost looked like the girl in the video.

I closed my laptop, found a fresh page in a notepad and a purple pen, and started to write.

'LITTLE BUT IMPORTANT THINGS.'

I ran through moments in my head that would spark any sort of joy in my heart and jotted them down, numbering them so I could count them up as a collection. On the surface they looked stereotypical; something you would read in a teen magazine, or on a relatable Tumblr page. But each of these things was a reminder of who I was, what made me happy, and a reason to live. I'd found myself again in 'opening a window when there's rain' and 'first kisses' and 'good books and the worlds you get lost in'.

I was the girl in the video. I had lived and loved in this bedroom and this world, and if I had been happy before, I could be happy again. I was still intact – despite feeling as though my brain had burned through my body and left me as an unrepairable skeleton. I had all the parts and resources to get back to a place where I could sing and dance around in a room with a friend again.

* * *

I woke up the next day feeling lighter. I crept around my flat, giving myself little tasks. I made myself breakfast and tea, I showered and moisturised my skin for the first time in a few days, I put on cotton clothes and opened the blinds. It was like the day after food poisoning – taking life in little bites, being cautious and gentle to myself, worried I was teetering on the edge of relapsing again. But I was okay.

I was just okay.

I went to a friend's picnic in the park in the evening and sat around with my friends, staring at my hands most of the night and wishing I could join them in the vivid world I seemed to have lost. We walked to the shops after the sun had set and while they babbled and skipped around each other, I hung back, staring at cars driving past and wondering if they were moving fast enough to knock me down. But I had gone outside. My friends had placed daisies on my head to make me giggle, pulling me by the hand and daring me to cartwheel on the damp evening grass. As a percentage, I probably felt 20% good and 80% terrible.

But I felt 20% good. And the next day I went on a waterslide with my mum and little sister, and I raced them down a hill, tripping over my feet and landing in a heap of limbs in a swimming costume, relishing in the sounds of my family laughing around me. And then the day after that I did a little bit of work, and over a few more days I managed to ease myself back into life, and I had days where I was far more than just okay, and I cried about the idea that I wouldn't have experienced the things I did if I hadn't held on.

There have still been times when I have crashed back into the same dark hole I was in during my breakdown, and I have sat and cried in the same spot on my floor as I did then. But then I bring out the list of little but important things, I climb into Hazel's bed for her to stroke my hair, and I remember the lessons I have learned since last hitting rock bottom; the main one being that I have been here before and I have got up and out of it every time.

LITTLE BUT IMPORTANT THINGS

1. Painted toenails + nails
2. three/four part harmonise I did myself
3. Working on a collab + nailing it
4. doddlevloggle audience
5. Sammy being stupid
6. A text from jón, lessa, rushy
7. Opening a window when there's rain
8. cats. Oh my god cats.
9. Everyone moving west! Evan! Lucy! Hannah + Lauren!
10. Swimming
11. hugs
12. First kisses
13. American tours!
14. A fucking ace cuppa tea
15. New bedsheets after a bath
16. Cheese
17. Newly cleaned + hoovered room
18. Good books + the worlds you get lost in
19. Cheesy af but seeing stars + realising ur tiny + yr head is tiny
20. The paper basket noise when deleting shit on macbook
21. getting recognised by a youtuber/creator I respect

LIST OF HAPPY

* Bare feet in a lift
* Wet mud and wellies
* Perfume from a few summers ago
* That 2011 tune (throw my hands up)
* Cold playground poles combined with a runny nose and fresh air
* Sound of planes in the sky
* Clusters of daisies in bright green grass
* The first glass of prosecco
* Sitting at the front on the top deck of a bus
* Bare sunshine
* A sympathetic back rub
* The 'pop' of opening a new jam jar
* Waking up to morning giggles and chatter after a sleepover
* Apples, honey and cinnamon combination
* Passionfruit lip balm from the Body Shop
* A friend-made cup of tea
* A borrowed unfamiliar but cosy jumper
* Cat's noses

Why can't I remember stuff? Time goes so quickly, days are over, I can't think or imagine anything anymore. I almost wish I have this thyroid thing so at least there's an explanation for my stupid brain.

I wish I could lie in bed and think again. How have I forgotten how to do that?

I should look over the happy list more.

YOU'RE PRETTY ENOUGH TO BE LIKED AND NICE ENOUGH TO HAVE FRIENDS

THE WORLD IS YOURS. AND FREE!

the 9 year old Dodie lives on!

YOU ARE YOUNG AND SAFE AND HEALTHY

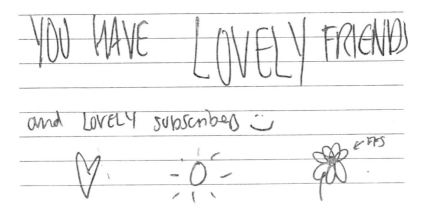

YOU HAVE LOVELY FRIENDS

and LOVELY subscribers :)

LUNCHTIME OR 4 A.M.

* You've just awoken from a twenty-minute nap, your eyes dry and heavy, your brain swollen. Noises are uncomfortable and cut through silence right through to the core of your brain. Time is wrong, and confusing; has it been a minute, or an hour, since that thing was said? It wouldn't be surprising if it was lunchtime or 4 a.m.

* The film you've been watching at the cinema has just ended, the credits are rolling, and suddenly you're trying to pull yourself back to reality. You exit the theatre and look around at your friends, trying to regain some familiarity. But they're not the characters you've been empathising with for the past few hours – they're solid and real, and, for some reason, weird-looking.

* It's the hottest day of the year so far and you've been lying on a towel in the garden, staring up at the blue sky and listening to the sounds of planes, breezes and the ice cream truck. You get up to go get a glass of fruit juice, head inside and suddenly your eyes don't work. Your pupils are struggling to dilate in time and your kitchen seems as though it's pitch-black; even though you technically can still see, everything has lost its clear outline and your vision is filled with fuzzy specks.

* It's your turn in the loo queue at a party, so you stumble in, clearly intoxicated, and try to lock the door with numb hands. Your face is buzzing and you giggle to yourself as you turn around and slam your hands on the basin, staring at someone in the mirror. They have scary eyes and a red mouth that's curved upwards, creating wrinkles that sink around the smile. You comb your hands through your hair and they copy. So you make a face, and their nose crinkles up, their eyebrows furrow and their eyes become blacker. Panic creeps up your chest as your mind struggles to compute the familiar stranger in the glass, their expression now turning cold.

Depersonalisation disorder, (DPD), or dissociation, or derealisation (DR), is described as the feeling of detachment from reality. Growing up, I had never heard of it, and so when it started to feel like I was dreaming all the time, I had no idea what was happening. I at first thought it was due to lack of sleep. Then I thought it was just what happens when you grow up; then I figured it was just depression, as I wasn't getting any joy or feeling whatsoever from activities any more. It took me a few years to find a Wikipedia page about it, and then I spent a good day crying about the idea that there were other people who felt like I did. I was officially diagnosed with depersonalisation earlier this year.

It affects me in different ways, one of which being my eyesight. The world looks flat and fake, and my peripheral vision seems very dark, or very light, as if I'm looking through a vignette filter. When I look at big buildings, or giant natural features of the world, like mountains and sunsets, they don't look real, and so rather than triggering admiration at beauty I feel overwhelmed by sadness and disappointment. DPD also affects my memory. I compare the sensation to feeling drunk (although it is different in many ways), and so in my dazed state I find it difficult to feel present and grounded in the moment, and unable to log time or experiences as clearly and easily as I used to. I constantly have to ask my friends about the moments we spent together, movies I've apparently seen, things I apparently said or did. Because of these symptoms, I also find that it causes depressive episodes and anxiety.

Travelling, parties, sunshine – things that would usually bring me joy now created confusion and disappointment.

Conversation was also met with panic – 'Can they tell I'm spaced out? Do they think I'm weird because I keep staring off into the distance? Did I say that already?' So I started to cancel outings and travelling opportunities to stay at home in a safe and familiar space, where I could be in a daze by myself and not worry about it too much. I spent a few years grieving the past, and the days of clarity, happiness and carelessness. It felt as if I was stuck like this forever, and that the only place in the timeline of my life when I felt okay was before any of it had seeped in.

I had read that the cause of my condition stemmed from deeply rooted trauma, and so I went on therapeutic journeys, processing losses and exploring my pain, desperately searching for where the source of the off switch for my brain was. I found out a lot, and I dealt with a lot. I became able to manage my depressive episodes a lot better, I healed over open wounds of broken friendships and insecurities, and I improved the way I dealt with being spaced out – but I still was, and am, very much, spaced out, all of the time.

Sometimes there isn't an obvious reason for something, and there isn't a simple solution, and that's okay. I will always keep looking for a way to feel awake again.

I'm currently undergoing TMS treatment (transcranial magnetic stimulation – google it!) and I have appointments booked to talk about medication and all my other options. Despite it being the third most commonly experienced psychological symptom, depersonalisation isn't talked about anywhere near enough.

It took me five years to get an official diagnosis, after multiple patronising doctors' appointments and a lot of confusion and pain. Since I found the name and I opened up about my experiences, I have had friend after friend reach out to me saying they know someone who's been feeling like they're dreaming all the time, or that during conversations they find their souls up on the ceiling rather than in their own body.

I don't know whether I'll ever feel present again, but until I find that out, there's not a lot I can do about it except look after myself and share my experiences to empathise with people who are also in the am-I-really-here? club.

And there are bright sides to it, if you look hard enough.

It helped me to write a great song. I made a wonderful friend through bonding over our mutual spaced-out-ness. And perhaps the most cool, DPD is a coping mechanism for high levels of stress. On a windy day in September I was booked to jump out of a plane as part of a presenting job, and I'd told the whole team that I'd never do it; but because I was so numbed to reality that day, I didn't feel anxiety to the overwhelming, restricting amount I usually would have if I felt present. Spacing out was my Dutch courage, and although I experienced skydiving differently as to how I would have if I wasn't depersonalised, at least I experienced it!

TRAVELLING AND DEPERSONALISATION

As I've mentioned, my DPD tends to worsen whenever I travel. I start to truly understand the meaning of depersonalisation; it is as if I am losing myself.

Here are two things I have written on my travels, during times when the feeling was overwhelming.

THAILAND

A twenty-year-old girl wearing polka-dot pyjama shorts, her damp hair in a tight yet messy bun, and a floaty, striped cropped top, leans out of her balcony in Thailand and looks up at the stars.

Her view of the world currently is a deep navy, almost black, sprinkled with silver, and a forest-green mountain of palm trees and leaves. The air is wet, thick, warm. A fan provides a constant breathy drone. Crickets boast to each other; light chatter from hotel staff is occasionally present, but mostly drowned out by a warm breeze.

The world is so beautiful. And her brain is not ugly, but just chilly. It aches, a little. She is unable to drink in the gorgeousness of her surroundings, despite her throat closing up with thirst for enlightenment. Her phone is full of snapshots as her eyes are unable to take any. Her notebook is stuffed with thoughts as her head is full of holes and they usually spill out.

She has been here before; not here, in Thailand, but far from 'home', in the dark, while other souls rest in blissful sleep. And, she has accepted, she will be here again.

Alive, but not alive.

Content, but not content.

The stars watch her sigh on her balcony.

MIRROR

It's 2.49 a.m. in the UK but goodness knows what time it is wherever we are in the world now. I managed to sleep for about two hours, but Evan's crackly snore woke me up so I put on Bridget Jones's Baby (wouldn't recommend, it's horribly cheesy) and tried to rehydrate my body from the many glasses of free wine I drank. How is the air in planes so dry?! I feel like my nostrils are trying to inhale sand.

Anyway, I just scared the heck out of myself. After chugging two bottles of water I naturally needed the toilet, so I squeezed past seats, through the tiny door, locked it, and sat on the loo. There's a mirror right next to where you sit, so I turned and studied my face for a bit.

Because of my depersonalisation, it's always weird to look in a mirror. I don't usually look at it too much, because it can get strange.

But I was curious, so I stared, up close, into a puffy-eyed, blotchy-skinned familiar face.

I stared a bit too long, actually.

Panic climbed up my back as I realised I was staring into the face of a possibly angry, wide-eyed, weird version of my brother. Or maybe my sister. The face was so familiar, yet completely foreign, and my mind screamed danger.

Now, as I'm sober, and not completely mad (yet), I obviously know that this was my face. And it is quite comical to imagine a jetlagged girl sitting on a plane loo, staring up close at herself in a mirror and murmuring 'what the fuck'.

But that was one of the weirdest experiences of my life. I felt as though there was another person inches away from my eyes.

It's okay. I know it was just a combination of my DPD/DR, two hours of confusing sleep and a very clean mirror. But holy heck – I almost want to go back and look again.

(The person in the mirror did not look great – they needed some ice on their eyes or something.)

MANAGING AND MANAGING (BY MANAGER JOSH)

'Snap out of it', 'It's going to be okay', 'Trust me, you'll be fine' – these are all the things you want to say but you simply can't. You're not relatable, you just don't understand.

The usual metaphor that people perceive life as is either 'Is the glass half empty or is it half full?' As an optimist I would go with the latter, but I can imagine Dodie's answer being something along the lines of 'The glass is on the floor; there's water everywhere', and it's with that unpredictable thought process that every day is a new challenge for me when considering her emotions and still getting the work completed.

Every day we pick up that glass, we clean the floor dry, and we do the best thing we can do to start us off. We talk. We talk deep. 'How are you feeling?' A general question that can be said so frivolously and carefree. However, we don't speak like that. We couldn't speak like that. Since working with Dodie I've come to realise just how important emotions and empathy really are.

Funny to think that, in a world of business, she's cynically seen as a 'product', yet I consider her more a 'friend'. 'How are you feeling?' now feels so complex and a question best put away in that emotional drawer and to be replaced with just 'MOR-NING' and then followed by the tasks at hand.

Depersonalisation was new to me, something I had never even heard of before I started working with Dodie. 'It feels like being drunk all the time' was one of the first things I remember her saying about it. This really stuck with me. How can something so sought after by the adults I see on the tube on a Friday night, or the friends out on a stag/hen-do be so awful to suffer from? Then I realised she said 'ALL. THE. TIME' and then it made sense. Those three words put directly at the end of that feeling sounded truly difficult and that's when my empathy really began.

Thinking through Dodie's comparison of being drunk opened my eyes more to the low points. When being drunk, things come at you in random blinks and flashes, you don't take things in like your sober self can, and your memory is the length and size of a garden pea. To know that someone who I'm close to has this feeling as part of their day-to-day life changed my whole ethos of how I would work as a manager.

I looked at Dodie then with her glazed-over eyes and unperturbed look on her face and thought I saw someone who wasn't paying attention; the information was going in but it wasn't sticking. Like a teenager in Latin class. What I realise now is that she's there, she's listening, she's taking it in, my English was never Latin, but there's something in the way in her brain and I need to work my way around it to help her in every way I can.

'Take a minute/day/week out, put all the work things aside if you need to. We will get there and it's still going to be brilliant, leave it with me,' I find myself saying to Dodie. This is because I take my duty of care more seriously than ever. I'm not dealing with a 'product' or with a 'cash cow', I'm dealing with a person. An incredible one. One who I know will get better with time and with love.

Joshua Edwards (Manager Josh), 2017

WATERY MILK (SUICIDAL)

I roll the idea around in my head like I would a boiled sweet in my mouth. It tastes of watery milk, and it numbs and coats my brain.

How sad. What a sad thought to be consumed by. A sad thing to find a small amount of hope in.

Of course I'm not feeling a lot, so my eyes do not well up. The heaviness of the idea tugs at the tissues in my chest, but not enough to rip them and cause me to bleed. There is no liquid. Perhaps it has all frozen inside.

I push my glasses up to my scalp for the tenth time that night, wondering again if I might be able to see better without them in front of my eyes. As if it is that easy to fix, and that's all I've been doing wrong this whole time. But it doesn't matter if I can see or not, for I'm not even in the room. The sounds around me are from another time, a different place. I am dreaming, I am floating, and if I stop digging my nails into the backs of my arms I will close my eyes and drift into the grey. I look around to closer objects, my vision clinging on to the threads of reality like a cardshop ribbon tied to a giant helium balloon.

My fingernails are familiar.

I look up, and I am gone again. The cycle begins. I drag my glasses out of my hair, and set them back on my nose. I move my body in time and stretch my lips out and yell out the words that usually make my head spin, or my lungs swell, or my stomach tingle, or s o m e t h i n g.

But all I taste is watery milk. The promise of sleep.

DEAR HAPPY

I missed you dearly,
thought I was nearly
there forever, at last together.

Is our time fleeting?
Is even meeting
a healthy idea, or am I getting too near?

Don't try to fight it,
I'm here for tonight,
and I'll be waiting for you
until we meet again.

I know it's scary
but don't be wary,
if we don't have that long
let's not waste it feeling wrong.

This isn't the end,
I'm your lifelong friend,
sure it's been a while
but I'll be here when you smile.

So don't try to fight it,
I'm here for tonight,
and I'll be waiting for you
until we meet again.

Would you mind staying?
It's getting late, but I will visit you soon
so try just to get through.
And don't try to fight it,
I'm here for tonight,
and I'll be waiting for you
until we meet again,
I'll be waiting for you
until we meet again.

HALF GOOD, HALF BAD

My Bad Brain demands to be dramatic. It feeds on attention, lying down with its arms twisted up in the air, its legs sprawled out, and an upturned frown and tears in its eyes. 'Oh, woe is me. Nothing will ever be good again.'

My Good Brain can never relate. It scoffs – nothing is ever as bad as Bad Brain makes it out to be. You can laugh at anything; just choose to see the funny. It doesn't understand why you would step into the dark place, wallow in it and not try to get out.

But Bad Brain knows that when you're okay, you're just treading water. And it's easier to just let go, and sink, down to where you belong; where you don't have to struggle or try; you just exist, naturally, in depression.

People experience their mental health problems in different ways, but for me, I flip back and forth between optimistic and utterly hopeless. Luckily I've got to a place now where I can recognise when I'm spiralling, and I know I should at least try to ignore the loud voice in my head that tells me this is all I am and will ever be. It's difficult to write this chapter, because my view of the truth changes with my mental state. I am an unreliable narrator, like Nick from *The Great Gatsby*. But if I am to believe one of the voices, I'd much rather it be the one that tells me I'm going to be okay, right?

* If you're feeling hella dramatic and completely consumed by your bad thoughts, try to pretend to be positive at least. Allow yourself some dramatic episodes, but then practise laughing about it. My flatmate, Hazel, and I have spent many a night awake at 4 a.m., hunching over toilets, shuddering through a terrible state of panic and depression. But we still managed to banter with the paramedics after Hazel mistook a panic attack for a near-death experience. We make jokes about our 'big trigs' (triggers) for episodes of bad mental states. Brains are weird, and sometimes the lies they spew are so ridiculous you have to laugh.

* Sometimes you've just got to ride these things out. You should be getting support from doctors, charities, therapy, medication and so on, but perhaps you're waiting on help, or none of these things work this time – remember, you will be okay. You WILL BE OKAY. This will absolutely not last forever. Take it from someone who was 100% convinced it would. So while you wait, distract yourself and don't feed it any more attention, even though it's shouting at you.

* Self-care, self-care, self-care. You will feel like there's absolutely no point in doing anything, because nothing will give you joy. But there will be tiny things that help, and all of these little things will add up to help you feel better. Listen to your body – if you feel like you can't handle a birthday meal at a restaurant tonight, then don't. You are 100% allowed to take a sick day, just as you would if you were stuck at home with a tummy bug. Of course there comes a point when you make yourself worse by not going outside. Give yourself tiny tasks: take a bath with your favourite mango soap, make hot cups of sweet tea, and, gosh, don't forget to eat reasonably. Your body won't work properly if you don't treat

it well, and so you can't expect your brain to either. When you can't find your purpose in a day, make it to look after yourself.

* Have you been alone for the past few days? Or have you constantly been around people all week? You might recognise yourself sinking when you haven't had the company or the space you personally need to feel okay. I also tend to feel a lot worse when I haven't slept properly, maybe from jetlag, or when I haven't had a break from working and stress for a long while. Your mental health problems can kick in any time, but sometimes there is an obvious reason to them, and you have to cut your brain some slack and give it what it needs.

* Don't give up hope! There's always another pathway you can take. You are learning and growing every day; think of the difference between you now and yourself from a few years ago. There is so much time for you to find out ways of helping yourself and techniques to deal with problems. Every time you hit rock bottom, you bring with you everything you've picked up from the last time you climbed up.

* As I have mentioned, for a long time I mourned the past because that was the only time I saw myself as happy. I knew it was pointless to hurt over that so much, because that's the one place you can't revisit; but nevertheless I wasted a lot of my late teens obsessing about how nothing would ever be as good as it was before. But through all of that, I learned that brains have a tendency to glorify memories. I still look back on all my experiences with a pang of sadness and a longing to return, even the times I know to have been awful. If you are like me, remember that one day you will look back on the time you are in

right now with that same sensation of yearning. Try to zoom out and view the situation for what it is, not for the terrible filter of unhappiness you might be looking through currently. Meditation and mindfulness can help you with this, to help ground you and notice each second you experience. Indulge in nostalgia now and again if you wish, but remember that the present moment will become the past, so you might as well enjoy it while you're in it.

obsessions

ADORED BY HIM

Pretty girl, with the butterscotch hair,
your eyes and the sunshine smile you wear,
I can see how you make his soul glow.

Pretty girl, with the adventurous mind,
you envision so much you make me look blind.
You spark his life in ways I'll never know.

I won't hate you
but oh, it stings.
How does it feel
to be adored by him?

Pretty girl, there's no need to fret,
cause it's midnight, he's drunk and you're the one in his head.
You don't even have to try at all.

Pretty girl, oh, he looks at you
as if life is perfect and the world is new –
in those moments I just feel so small.

I won't hate you
but oh, it stings.
How does it feel
to be adored by him?

How stupid to think
that I could compare
to the pretty girl
with the butterscotch hair.

IF YOU ASK HER TO LISTEN,
SHE MIGHT GIVE YOU A LOOK.

SCROLL. DRINK. SHRINK

I wrote this six months ago about a friend I once knew. There was a boy involved, and it all got a bit strange and uncomfortable, so we kindly cut ties and said goodbye and good luck. We were smart about it and treated each other with care, but breaking contact with a soul I enjoy to know is never something I have done well.

And so I didn't.

Every now and again I'd just have a little check, to see what she was up to. Maybe once a week. And then it was every couple of days or so. And then it was every day, and her face turned into something different in my brain. It was probably a mixture of the involvement of the boy, my bad mental state at the time, and the fact that I 'wasn't supposed' to be doing this, but over a few weeks it had twisted into an unhealthy obsession. I know I tend to get addicted to anything very easily: I tap my head five times whenever I think about death, I bite the skin around my nails religiously, and pick at anything on my scalp and back, and whenever I approach the idea that I could train myself to stop these bad habits there is a loud voice that laughs, and shouts 'AS IF!'. And so I continued to stalk; ignoring the warning signs flashing in my brain and friends who widened their eyes and shook their heads when I confided in them.

This is embarrassing to share. I feel shame when I read the thoughts I had and the things I did, but comparison is human, and this is something I know a lot of people struggle with.

Will I ever stop typing your name into the Instagram search bar?

Will I ever stop logging into my secret account to watch you beam and babble on your Snapchat?

Am I in love with you? Am I jealous? Are you really as wonderful as my brain tells me you are, and, if so, how do you exist and how am I not allowed to know you?

I don't know why it aches so much. And I don't know what will ever make it go away. I don't even understand what I want from you.

My eyes run up and down your face and body, flipping between admiration and intrigue – trying to find a possible way that anyone could ever see you as anything but beautiful. You are honestly like a princess; gentle and delicate, pretty and pastel.

You inspire me. You make me want to write like you. To be colourful like you. To dance and twirl and radiate like you.

But.

You make me want to starve, to look like you. To always look like you, and when I don't, it hurts. I can't swap my acne for your freckles, or my wonky smile for your neat white one, and the more I look at you with adoration the more disgust for myself seeps in.

It's strange. You can't be perfect. You must feel as though you have a bad angle for your face that you are cautious to never show, or maybe funny-shaped feet that make you feel anxious about wearing sandals. I want to know about them; but is that because I want to help you feel better about yourself and bond over insecurities, or because I'm so desperate to discover anything about you that is in the slightest bit ugly?

It's every single day.

And it's so easy to find you. There's so much of you. Is that why you do it?

I typed in your name for perhaps the tenth time today. I scrolled, drank, sank, as usual. I very nearly liked a picture, by accident, and my heart dropped to my stomach.

Of course, half of me wishes I did. So you could see. I just want you to understand. And I want to be as special as you.

* * *

This lasted for a while. I continued to compare myself and I poured so much energy into running over brain patterns of 'I am not good enough', feeling trapped in a terrible cycle of a short burst of satisfaction, comparison, self-hate and then guilt. I'd clear my search history again and again, but always find my way back to typing her name into the search bar, just as I'd attack my newly healed hands with another session of nibbling.

Luckily, it came to a peak, and then eased off naturally. Going cold turkey clearly didn't work for me, and so in little steps I practised not thinking about it, diverting my attention away from social media and being much kinder to myself every time I was too curious to stop. The obsession and fascination slowly faded away, and although I'd still take a little peek every now and again, the ugly thoughts had blossomed into ones of admiration and casual interest. Rather than hurting over our differences, I started to be proud of them; while also starting to notice and enjoy our similarities as well. The flames died down, and she settled back into my head as just someone I used to know.

And then something wonderful happened. I tried out looking at myself in the way I used to look at her. I looked at my own Instagram, my videos, my art, and I noticed that I too was special, and beautiful. I also put smiles on people's faces. I love the way my nose looks when I laugh and it scrunches up; my stomach is not entirely flat because I am proud to be a healthy woman; I give a heck of a lot of love away to the people I care about; and I am deep-thinking, objective and empathetic.

It wasn't that I became any more magical, or she any less. My insecurities were still very much there, and everything I admired about her was too. But we levelled out in my brain, both to 'human'. And both to 'imperfect'. And both to 'wonderful'.

For a long time I was desperate to be someone else. I didn't realise that was what it was – but you cannot be happy with yourself if you desire to swap every feature inside and outside yourself that you don't like with someone else's. You must love yourself first, and learn that only you can give what you have given to the world – and that makes you special.

And then you can admire people and become inspired by them, and borrow things that you like as an extension for your already amazing existence.

16 Feb 12

It's times like these where I am very glad to have a diary.

Musical Bethan. Bethan leadly.
I am so jealous of you.   24th June LOL.
You have clear skin. A cute small nose,
Lovely hair, a lovely voice, beautiful
body, boobs, long eyelashes, big eyes.
etc.   HAHA MARCH 2013

I could go on.
I'm becoming obsessesed, I seriously
am. For Gods sake Dodie, she's
just a girl!?!!.
Feels like I'm in love with her :
But seriously.
She's so beautiful.

*Although this section I've written for the book isn't about Bethan, I wanted to show that even at the age of sixteen I was comparing myself to someone else.

FORKFULS OF SALAD

You're seven, and you're holding a smooth stick-like plastic Barbie, sprouting bright blonde hair from her tiny head. You pinch her waist between your forefinger and thumb, and hold her sharp shoulders in your hands.

You're thirteen, and you're reading *Mizz* magazine. They tell you how to get ready for a date by choosing a denim mini skirt, pairing it with a cute tee and some lip gloss, and you stare at the pink girl with a crop top and a bare, flat tummy.

You're fifteen, and you're watching cartoons where every female character has collarbone lines etched in, their necks and heads separated by a carved jawline.

You're seventeen, and you're scrolling down Tumblr. You drink in grey images of thin skin on bones peeking out from oversized jumpers, ruffled socks that hang loose on legs that look like tent poles with tags that read #beautiful #girl #art #cute #sexy.

* * *

From an early age we are taught that there is no other option; if you want to feel beautiful then you must be skinny. You might get the odd chubby character now and again, but it's outweighed by the overall imagery of tiny women with no rolls or the natural tub that sits over your womb to protect your reproductive system. If a picture showing those features is posted, it's seen as a statement – an idea, a wish of what we want to be seen as beautiful.

So when we are brainwashed to believe what seems to be 'The Truth' – that you must have long, skinny arms and legs, a visible collarbone, no natural fat under your jaw or on the lower half of your stomach, to match anyone who is on TV or in magazines or the female characters from cartoons – you start to believe that if you don't have that, you are ugly. It is wrong, and you feel shame.

Don't tell me my eating disorder is for 'vanity' when I am surrounded by a world that is shouting at me to BE SMALLER.

* * *

The obsession with calorie counting and the promises I'd make to myself – not to eat until the evening, or to throw up the pasta I'd stuffed myself with – became so loud and rude in my head that on my US tour in 2016, I took the opportunity of an unfamiliar environment to start from scratch, and not eat. We'd stop off at a restaurant in the afternoon for a late breakfast and my eyes would immediately jump to the salads and soups on the menu. If there was nothing like that, I'd order eggs and toast, or the lightest sandwich I could find, and nibble and pick until it looked appropriate for me to push it away. I'd count my meals up in my head in hundreds, never allowing myself to reach a thousand per day, and I'd get into bed, my stomach aching and my pride glowing. The pounds dropped off me, and within a month I'd almost lost a stone. My arms stuck out of my body like twigs and my skin pulled tightly around my ribs, and I convinced myself that I was enjoying it. I took pictures of myself with my arms raised in the air so everyone could see my tiny waist, but when I was alone my arms were wrapped around my stomach, hands squeezing the fat that still remained, my mind screaming 'more'.

My friends would sip sodas and I'd wonder how they could ever waste calorie room on liquids. I would accidentally eat a few sweets before realising they'd amounted to what a more filling dinner could have been, and I'd walk around with hot guilt and anger at my carelessness, insisting with a fake smile that 'honestly, I'm stuffed'. I'd got used to the fact that standing up made me light-headed, and I'd wait a while for my vision to return before catching up with everyone who'd already danced away. The calorie-counting shouts in my head got louder, and I'd wake up with yesterday's score flashing red in my head: 'NOT GOOD ENOUGH. DO BETTER.'

We went to the beach one day, and I wore shorts and a crop top. I was half embarrassed about my ribs sticking out – terrified that someone would notice – and half smug, secretly slightly hopeful that someone would ask me if I was okay. We took pictures jumping over waves (until I had to go lie down in the sand, walking back slowly so that the blood didn't drain out of my head) and I scanned through them, deciding which to upload. In one of them I looked terrifyingly tiny, and it excited me. So I put them all up.

'Did you lose weight? Are you alright?'

'I don't wanna sound like a downer but I'm concerned, are you eating healthy? You look underweight?'

'Am I the only one who is worried because she is so thin?'

My stomach squirmed and I swallowed dryly, my breathing quickening. There was the most perfect amount of concern. Just a few tweets. I envisioned the small spoonfuls of scrambled eggs and nibbles of toast I'd had late that morning, and congratulated myself on my work.

And then . . .

'DODIE you have the most perfect little waist I'm so jealous.'

'This is the CUTEST! . . . also your figure is my all-time goals.'

'I wish a had a body like yours.'

My heart sank and the back of my neck became hot. I had an audience of mostly young girls, and I had just blasted their timelines with posed pictures of a smiling skeleton. They would be studying my stomach the exact same way I studied the Pinterest tag 'skinny', and now they would perhaps be taking second looks at their meals of choice. It wasn't that being skinny was terrible; nor was being large, or any other size at all. But society favours a smaller torso, and I had contributed to that, showing off a body for the wrong reasons, with girls logging my weeks of hunger as 'goals'.

Turns out starving yourself does not make you happy, ever. Your insecurities will not change with your dress size; they cannot be shaved off along with your baby fat, because they actually sit much deeper in your head. Furthermore, if you aren't fuelling your body and your brain properly, you will sink deeper into obsession and discontent because you won't have the tools or energy they need to pull you out of it.

* * *

So. It would appear to be that the answer to this, for me, is to shout back at the world that screams at me to be smaller.

What's the use in strengthening the side that favours stomach pains, guilt, obsessive counting and panic? As well as judgement, jealousy and self-hate. Well, of course, as I mentioned before, it's difficult to escape the vicious cycle, and we're rather unfairly outsized (lol) by the media and society. But when friends and strangers watch me chew on a couple of forkfuls of salad for half an hour, I'm joining the world's screams.

Here's how I can start. I will try to ignore the voices in my head that tell me I'm ugly. Before I shower, I will stand up straight in the mirror, and smile at my beautiful self.

Look at me! My clever, gorgeous body is bursting with life. There's a heart behind that ribcage that's dancing and contracting every second. I will look at myself the way I look at my best friend; when they worry about finding romance I know that there will be someone in the world who will adore every feature they have the way I do. I will make that someone me, and make my best friend also me. I should and can worship myself.

Let me tell you a secret: very few people will stand side on in the mirror and see their tummy as a flat line. The Instagram pictures you and I stare at and compare ourselves to were taken in the morning with a shrunken stomach and were handpicked from a bunch of poses. Our goal should be to be strong, not to be tiny, because let me tell you from personal experience, we cannot achieve true happiness from limiting our calories.

RAINBOW POISON

Green, pink, chocolate, blue,
why do colours of poison look so good?
Here's fun in a glass; drink it up now.

More bubbles, smooth but sharp,
gulp it down like oxygen in the dark.
There, it'll make you feel alive; drink it up now.

And I didn't want the night to end,
this liquid is my best friend,
I didn't want the night to end, no.

Look at me! I'm on top of the world
– goodbye, strings, I'm a pretty girl.
And now I know I've gone too far; drink it up now.
Green, pink, chocolate, blue
– why is rainbow poison so bad for you?
And now I know I've gone too far; drink it up now.

And I didn't want the night to end,
this liquid is my best friend,
I didn't want the night to end, no.

OVERDRINKING

Oh dear. Oh dear, oh dear, oh DEAR.

Well, you're pretty sure you're still drunk. You just about manage to pull your eyelids apart despite them practically being glued together from last night's mascara and sleep gunk. You're still in last night's clothes; your bra is cutting into your ribs; and the smell of smoke and beer from your dress is already making you gag. But are you going to throw up? You hope to God not.

Your mouth feels like an old carpet and your head and heart are pounding. You sit up, and the room lurches around you.

Yep. You absolutely are going to throw up.

You do your business, and it's absolutely horrible. You lie on the toilet bowl after heaving out the rainbow poison from your insides, and you start to cry (or laugh). Honestly, it could be either.

You tiptoe to the kitchen and pour yourself a glass of water. It slips down and cools your burnt throat, but it sits heavy in your raw stomach and threatens to rise up again. You creep back to your room, hunched over so as not to stretch out your tummy, and you strip out of the disgusting clothes that are hurting you and clamber back into the covers, luxuriating in the feeling of soft, loose material over your skin. You plug your dead – screen cracked, great, wonder when that happened? – phone in to charge, and lean over to grab a face wipe to scrub off the hardened black from your eyelashes. Your phone lights up after a few minutes, and then your heart sinks when you find the missed calls and angry messages from confused friends.

'Babe where did you go?? xx'

You don't actually know that, yet.

There are incoherent messages sent to random friends and a lot of question marks as replies. Your Twitter notifications are full of patronising slanty-faced emojis and 'look after yourself please!' replies to flash photos and embarrassing tweets, and it makes you angry, but not because they're wrong. Because they are very right. You royally fucked up.

Your life and body are in shutdown mode. Today is a sick day, a time out you shouldn't have needed to take. Your body is well and truly poisoned, and now you also have to deal with the shame that your intoxicated body unempathetically shoved towards future you. Everything feels terrible, and you mutter the words you believe with every fibre in your body, and yet somehow none of them at the same time: 'I am never drinking again.'

But you probably will, and that's okay. You can learn from yourself to make sure you don't do certain others things again, though!

If this is happening a lot, and you find it difficult or even impossible to say no to another drink when you're out, then have a little look at drinkaware.co.uk/selfassessment, or visit your GP for a little chat. There are a lot of different unhealthy relationships with alcohol, and although you might not fit in the stereotyped box, that doesn't mean it's not legit. If this sort of thing is happening to you every month or more then it's definitely time to start seeking help.

I've been here about four times in my life since I started drinking, and the episodes have become further and further apart; because each time it happens, I clean myself up and then re-evaluate everything. Why did I do that? At what point did I go wrong, and how can I not do that again?

First things first, though. It's self-care day for your poor body. The first time I was this hungover I googled various phrases like 'how to stop alcohol poisoning nausea' and 'what should I eat when I'm hungover'. I nibbled at ginger biscuits and downed Pepto-Bismol but nothing seemed to stop the need to throw up, so I reached out to one of the 'popular girls' from my school, desperate to know what to do.

'This is so random and I'm not even sure if it's okay to ask this but I've still got a lot of alcohol in my system so I'll blame my weirdness on that!

You know on Friday you were pretty drunk? When you woke up the next morning, how did you stop feeling so bad? I drunk FAR too much last night, and all I want to do is chunder :/ will it make me feel better or do I hold it in?

Hellllp, I feel like shit

Sorry, love you! <3'

(Excuse the use of the word 'chunder' – it was 2011.)

She replied:

'Awwww dodie! Nonono do NOT hold the sick in! Let it all out because then it's getting out of your system, I'm never usually sick when I'm drunk, but one time I was awful and paralytic, and I was sick like every 5 minutes. It was awful! Just every time you feel like chundering, let it all out! And drink plenty of water have water next to you all day, and just get rest bubby! You'll be fine! I love you! <3'

Well, I read that and then immediately ran to the toilet, where I remained for most of the day.

If you're particularly bad and you have truly ruined your insides, then she was right – it's best to get it all out. It's only going to sit in your stomach otherwise, and if your body's trying to tell you something then you should probably go along with it.

Water might make your tummy feel terrible, but you are most likely incredibly dehydrated. Take little sips if you can't deal with big gulps, and suck on ice cubes or frozen lollies. Nibble bits of toast, try a banana, and, honestly, you'll just have to ride it out. If you have a kind friend who is willing to rub your back and make you laugh at your moans and groans, call them up and get them to bring round fizzy lemonade and playing cards for distraction.

Once you've dealt with your body, it's time to deal with your brain and the mess of your life after a night of mistake making and carelessness.

I was lucky in that, instead of being angry, my parents pitied me and laughed at my mistakes, which certainly helped with the healing and learning process. They, however, didn't hold back from letting me know that the whole situation was absolutely entirely my fault. Don't get me wrong, sometimes there are valid reasons behind it all; whether that's first learning how to drink, or being incredibly sad to start with and losing any sight of self-care. But mostly that lack of care is just laziness, and regardless of whether there's a trigger or not, who was the one who decided on another cocktail? It was you!

So, if you fucked up last night, take responsibility for your actions. 'I'm so sorry, I was very drunk!' is not a good enough apology. 'Hey, there was a reason why I got so drunk, but that doesn't excuse the way I treated you last night. I'd like to apologise for . . .' is better. Like I said before, though, if you notice this behaviour is becoming a pattern, and you change completely when you drink, rather than just being a little careless, make sure you look into that. This advice is for the mistake makers, not the seriously struggling.

Now it's time to put down your sick bowl and pick up your thinking cap. What went wrong from this terrible, terrible experience, and how can we learn?

My first lessons went along the lines of this:

* Never, EVER drink on an empty stomach. NO exceptions.

* Don't mix your drinks. Also, never red wine again.

* Always take a charger for your phone.

Once I'd got the hang of what I was putting into my body, it then became a matter of how much:

* Check in with yourself when everyone is getting another drink and you feel the pull for more. If you're happily intoxicated, choose water. Drinking more will not maintain this feeling, it will worsen it.

* Three wines is always too much. One bottle between two people will end badly.

And very recently:

* Vodka jelly shots are VERY deceiving.

Then it was dealing with being drunk:

* Never ever use social media. You lose your apprehension for risky actions and that feeling is there for good reason.

* Don't send that long text. Type it out in your notes app and save it for tomorrow.

* Don't do the sex. Just don't.

Even after all of this, I won't be surprised if I end up there again, but if I do, I won't feel too bad about it. Everyone makes mistakes now and again, and, despite my writing a chapter in a BOOK sharing all of what I have learned so far about drinking, I am still just a human being, and so are you.

But the next time my eyes dart to another glass of Sauvignon blanc, I might just give the beginning of this chapter a re-read.

AN EXPERIMENT

TAKE ONE

DRINK ONE – a single whisky and Coke

It's 3.47 p.m. and I'm sitting in a business class lounge in South Korea. I've stuffed myself on sweet pumpkin sandwiches and shrimp fried rice, gulped bottled water all throughout the day, and for some reason, despite the early rise this morning, I'm in such a wonderful mood. Yesterday I stomped around Tokyo with my lip pouted, a crumpled frown on my face and a grey cloud over my head, but today there's a giggle in my throat and honey in my blood. I have about an hour until we're ready to board our flight, and there's a rack stacked with bottles of vodka, whisky, sake and champagne. There's also an open bar on the flight, and I've got nothing to do for the next fifteen hours but write.

So, I thought I'd combine the two. I've poured myself a syrupy sweet glass of whisky and Coke, and I'm taking little sips through a yellow straw I plucked from a thoughtfully placed glass. I'm going to document the thoughts and feelings that flow through my brain as booze flows through my blood. I guess I'm expecting these posts to become less coherent and the writing to probably worsen as I become more intoxicated. We will see!

The first drink is always the nicest. Since my break from alcohol in February, I've enjoyed the newly found ability to stop here. My smile widens, my head tingles and my mood eases. (I just tried to type 'easens' as a word. I'm clearly getting slightly more buzzed as I'm typing.) My demeanour warms and softens, and there's a little something that gives my curiosity a slight push. I tell someone I like their jacket; I take a picture of myself and say I like it; and I hold someone's hand without the nervous barrier in my head.

I asked my friend Evan to take a picture of me just now and I told him what I was doing. He smirked and told me he'd love to help out, and has just returned with two (much stronger than my original, might I add) drinks. I've noticed that there's an incredibly encouraging culture when it comes to alcohol, which is odd, when you think about alcohol as technically a poison. Luckily my friends are mostly not the pushy type, and I don't struggle with saying 'no, thank you' when I know I don't want something. But throughout my five years of drinking I've definitely found that people put a lot of shame on someone refusing another drink. I guess people want to glorify consumption so that drinking more makes you a hero, rather than an addict.

There is absolutely an urge for another drink.

* * *

(Okay, ironically I couldn't continue my experiment on that day. Alcohol causes deep-rooted emotions to rise to the surface, and so Evan and I ended up talking for hours and crying about our lives. We then both zonked out completely on the plane. Ha, bless me for having a constructed plan, adding alcohol and thinking it would work. I'll try again in a couple of days.)

* * *

TAKE TWO

I'm home, and my gal pal Lucy is coming over in about thirty minutes for wine, chats and good pasta. Let's see how this goes. What I'm immediately noticing is how excited I am to drink. I love alcohol.

* * *

(AGAIN. This didn't work out. We had wine, chats and good pasta, and I didn't want to write at all. If we're looking at lessons to learn from this, it's that booze can mess up your plans.)

* * *

TAKE THREE

ALRIGHT, THIRD TIME LUCKY. I'm yet again on another plane, the alcohol is free, and I have nothing else to do except sit in my seat for the next eight hours. I'm with Evan again, but we're both in a great mood, and I'm ready to drink and write. Here we go!

So I'm on drink one. I've accidentally spilled whisky and Diet Coke all down my seat and so I'm sitting on top of a wad of napkins; I've also only had five hours' sleep, and yet I'm so happy. Evan and I are babbling away about the videos we've filmed together and honestly it hasn't been this easy to laugh in SO long. There's a constant lightness in my chest that rises up to my throat and stretches across my cheeks and I'm just so HAPPY, and full of love. Everything is possible – I'm excited for the future! I'm suddenly thinking about where I'm going to live in the next few years. I could go anywhere I wanted; my life could be so different. I have friends; such wonderful, beautiful, incredible friends, and I'm so lucky to know them. I want to write a letter to myself, a reminder for when I'm sad and I don't feel like this; this is your norm. This is what you're meant to feel, because life is wonderful. It's exciting, it's fun, and depression lies to you! There is no truth in sadness, and there is no deep, dark hole in your brain that will forever be the base of your being. You are not treading water for happiness; you could be on a lilo, if you only chose your truth that life is happy.

* * *

DRINK TWO

Now, alcohol can heighten your emotions. I've noticed that when I'm depressed and I drink, I indulge those negative thoughts even more, and suddenly that is my truth. I'm always writing little messages and notes in my phone, determined to let my sober self understand this new revelation that is apparently 'the truth'. The real truth is the brain is bizarre, and we choose what the truth is. We are the only ones who can hurt our feelings, or our brain and body – your thoughts turn into emotions, which can either hurt or pleasure you. ANYWAY, I'm on my second drink, and my deep thinking is kicking in. My bladder is starting to feel full, my head is extremely heavy (perhaps I'm a lightweight), but I feel wonderful. This is absolutely the peak of my drinking, and my body and brain tells me that I must have MORE to maintain this beautiful feeling. My eyes have difficulty focusing, my mouth, teeth, tips of my fingers and toes feel numb, and there's still that flutter in my chest. I just don't care any more. It's interesting to recognise why making bad decisions is so common when you're intoxicated; it's because nothing matters. When you're sober, there are walls that you have to get through when you have a thought. Is this a good idea? What are the consequences? Can you deal with them? Do you really want this? When you have alcohol in your blood, those walls drop, and all you can see is the question and how much you want to answer it. You wave the walls away with a 'I can deal with all of that later' and a 'oh, I'll forgive myself'. I'll message someone I've been thinking of a lot, I'll post a sassy tweet because I think it's funny, I'll have another shot of tequila because, fuck it, I'm having fun. It's time to have a massive drink of water.

* * *

DRINK THREE

Luckily, over my years of drinking, I've managed to recognise the urge to 'just fuck it' and check in with myself. It's usually now that it's make or break for this sort of thing. The heaviness in my head moves to my eyes, and it's time to put down whatever drink I'm on and pick up water instead. I used to have to actively pull away from the attraction of more alcohol, but now I know that it's time to stop, and I've learned that I'll thank myself in the morning if I ask for a tap water now rather than another gin and tonic. To be honest, I don't like drink three, and I never have. For this experiment I took it, and I would when I was younger, but now I know that the fun is over and I'll only feel worse. I used to experience a lot of shame around not having another drink – people would spot me sipping water and moan, offer me another one for free, dance around me until I gave in, but . . . I think I said this earlier on? (Gosh, I'm drunk. I have no idea if these sentences mean anything.) I'm better at knowing and looking after myself. On drink three time is blurred, and suddenly I'm not thinking about the future any more. Or the past. Or even the present.

I'm so out of it that experiences and feelings and senses are washing over me, and I'm floating through time. This is why I compare DPD to feeling drunk – being drunk is just that to an extreme.

Alcohol is still exciting to me, because it stretches your brain and allows you to indulge in the thoughts you forget or try not to think about. It weakens guards, it encourages, it pumps through. But it should be treated like chocolate, or Christmas. It should be a treat, because you're actually poisoning your body to feel like this. It is so normalised in British culture; I used to drink every day, convinced that it was completely natural to do so. But I don't want to be like that! I don't want to feel this three-drinks-in slump every day. I want to practise happiness without the fuel of booze, and I want to be healthy, well rested and hydrated.

It's been around four hours since I started to drink, and I'm tired. I want to sleep, and I feel stupid. I'm worried about how I'll feel when I wake up. Did I say anything stupid? Luckily this time I haven't been online as I've been on a plane, but in the past my 'fuck it' attitude would have inspired me to post something I didn't really mean online. If I'm home, I'll down as much water as I can, scrub my face haphazardly with soap, and clamber into bed, falling asleep instantly.

Evan is currently zonked out from his red wine; his head is tilting back, his mouth is hanging open, and his chest is rising and falling slowly.

I'm still happy. I'm going to ask for some more water and sleep too. I'll update you in a few hours. :)

* * *

AFTER A NAP

I usually have difficulty sleeping on a plane, but as I was drugged and sleepy from the whisky it wasn't too hard to pass out. I definitely went over the amount I usually want to consume, because whenever I closed my eyes, my brain spun around in my skull and my stomach lurched as if I was being thrown around on a rollercoaster. But luckily that didn't last too long, and I think I slept for about two hours. Although I feel a little queasy, I'm luckily still in high spirits (as in joyful – I'm pretty sure I've sobered up).

Alright! What have we learned here?

I had some rather surprisingly coherent thoughts, despite being on drink three, that pretty much summed up the way I feel about alcohol. Drinking is incredibly normalised where I grew up, and in a lot of other places in the world, and although I would argue that if it is treated responsibly it is mostly harmless, it doesn't hurt to check in and question what it is to you. I am now at a place where alcohol is a good, but little, thing in my life.

My flatmate pours me a glass of wine some evenings and we sit on the sofa and sip and natter. I sit cross-legged on hot dry grass and enjoy a strawberry cider in the summer sun. And every few months or so, I'll have two gin and tonics and a spontaneous tequila shot, which I'll regret when I crawl into bed after downing a full glass of water and licking leftover salt off the back of my hand, head and stomach spinning. I have mostly learned not to reach for drink three if I am consuming alcohol, thanks to a few terrible life lessons, and I'm interested to know how my relationship with alcohol will change as I get older too.

It's definitely interesting to read back my intoxicated thoughts. I feel inspired by my tipsy brain. If my brain has the potential to be that excited, then it can absolutely do it without the need for alcohol. There are clearly walls put up against spontaneous ideas for a reason – let's message my ex! Yes, I WILL miss the last train home, sleep on your floor and wake up extra early tomorrow! – but there's a middle ground to be found. Sometimes on my tipsy adventures I have reached out to old friends and then gone for a coffee a few days later for a well overdue catch-up and a reminder that they are an important person in my life. Other times I have written lyrics about topics I haven't dared to address in my mind, and then found them months later while scrolling down voice memos and used them for inspiration.

I'm starting to get a headache. Time for more water.

Tomorrow, after I have landed, slept and readjusted to UK time, I will start to ask, without the use of alcohol, 'WWTDD?' What Would Tipsy Dodie Do?

Hopefully it'll result in a random phone call with my grandma, or a walk to town to get a cheese toastie, or a realisation that the future is actually exciting. There is a me who can appreciate her life to the fullest – and she doesn't need any whisky for it.

I need;
- * start fake tanning maybe not.
- * new clothes
- * new haircut (search around)
- * dye hair? Red?
- * Clinique foundation?
- * change eyes- eyeliner on top?
- * if not haircut, do wavey hair every morning!
- * PERFUME.

I WILL CHANGE!
- * Shave all of the time. Everywhere.

Stuff it, let's write more.

I need to • keep my hair volumed
perm? Fringe? Layers?
- • Sort out my skin
- • SPRAY perfume whenever you can
- • WEAR NICE CLOTHES.

PAINT

When I was in year eleven, I wrote my English-speaking essay on why anyone should be allowed to wear make-up and not get criticised for it. I was angry at the hypocrisy of society; in school, make-up was banished, but in adulthood and work it was expected and professional. I was dealing with deep insecurities around my face and skin (which you can probably see shine through the lyrics) and I felt passionate about the idea that I should have been allowed to help myself feel better through expression. If we were taught that make-up wasn't a mask, and that it was neither needed nor shameful, perhaps we would all have felt a lot better about ourselves a lot sooner.

PAINT

Am I hiding, or is this just me?
Am I not allowed to be who I want to be?
It makes me feel better, cause pretty I ain't!
What's wrong with a little bit of paint?

Am I being looked down upon again
cause I'm wearing this lipstick in shade number ten?
'You look like a panda, with that black around your eyes!'
Oh yes, you're completely right; it's all part of my disguise . . .

You wouldn't put down a boy with scars
from an operation that he had in the past.
He wears baggy jumpers to cover them up;
he's not too happy in his skin. Just like us!

I can't draw a thing but you could call this art;
applying blusher doesn't make me a tart.
Don't call her an orange, cause I think that's unkind,
and if you don't like Lady Gaga, that's your problem, not mine.

And I'm not saying every face is a canvas,
I'm just saying if you're feeling anxious
you should be able to wear whatever you choose,
and if you think that I'm wrong, well – I refuse!

SKIN

People are kind, and sometimes they draw me. I am used to seeing my face sketched in different ways: some naturalistic, some cartoon-like. Mostly I am drawn a little skinnier than I actually am, with a teeny nose and big eyes. They might add in freckles, but I am always drawn with clear, soft skin and a healthy complexion.

At an event in the US, a smiley person gifted me with a little watercolour drawing, boarded with yellow card. They had dotted tiny splotches of pink along my cheeks, to match the actual acne scarring I carry with me in real life, and I was honestly the most flattered by that drawing of me that I'd ever been.

My skin problems started as soon as I hit puberty. I was so used to never having to think about my skin at all to dealing with giant lumps on my nose and forehead. I had always picked my newly healed scabs on my knees after falling over in the playground, and now that my entire face was covered in unfamiliar imperfections, I sat in front of my bedroom mirror, squeezing, dabbing with wet loo roll, and then plastering my skin in random products from the bathroom like toothpaste and Savlon in a desperate attempt to heal my broken skin. I had absolutely no idea what I was doing. Adults would just bat my hands away from creeping up to my face, hissing 'don't pick!' as if the compulsion was optional. All I wanted was for my face to feel clean and smooth, so I bought medicinal-looking exfoliators and pretty much scrubbed my skin red raw with hot water until it squeaked. I'd rub myself dry and enjoy a face that felt matt and clean, like it used to. Moisturiser sounded like a dumb idea. Why would I grease my face up again if I'd just cleaned it? So I'd take around a compact powder in my bag, and as my face got slimier in the day I'd drag a powdered-up cotton pad over my damaged skin.

So, yes, now I am covered in scars. At twenty-two years old, I look after my skin as best I can. Well, you'd think I'd have learned my lesson about picking, but that seems to be something engrained into me that I really battle against. I still squeeze spots before I go to bed and make my face bleed in public when I scratch at my imperfections absentmindedly on the train, when I'm lost in thought. But now after I've cleansed my cheeks and T-zone softly, I rub a little Vitamin E oil into my hands and smooth it over skin that is absolutely covered in little red marks.

It's alright; I'm okay with it now. A little bit later in my teens, when I was having sleepovers with my gal pals, we'd all change into our PJs after gossiping until the evening and get ready for bed. My friends would natter away while casually dissolving away their foundation with a face wipe, laughing carelessly and walking around barefaced, revealing fresh, clear skin. I would wait until the last possible moment in the night, and then slip away to the bathroom alone to wash my face and squeeze my spots as usual. Once I'd finished with my (terrible) skin-care routine, I'd dig out the secret foundation that I'd stashed in my wash bag and slather a thin layer onto my just cleansed skin. I'd go back into the room, pretending I too was fresh-faced like all of my clear-skinned friends, but still not able to look any of them in the eye.

I think, looking back, everyone knew, but we all pretended for my sake that they didn't. Of course, sleeping with my face coated in paint didn't exactly help with my acne, but it felt worth it at the time. I couldn't bear walking around without anything covering up what felt like angry mountains on my forehead.

But even with a thick layer of make-up on, around friends or strangers I was convinced that everyone was staring at it and thinking about it as much as I was. It felt like I had a sign on my face that read something like 'DON'T MENTION IT EVEN THOUGH YOU CAN'T STOP LOOKING AT IT', and so I'd walk around with as much hair in my face as possible, looking down in conversation when I noticed whoever's eyes I was talking to flicker to the particularly bad bit on my chin. I couldn't stand the idea that they were staring at me the way I would in the mirror – analysing every lump and scab, horrified, and immediately labelling me as ugly. I just knew that the first thing I looked at whenever I was talking to someone was their skin, and how much smoother and more matt it was than mine.

One day my pretty friend came into school with her hair covering the side of her face. She seemed upset. She spoke softer and littler than usual, and in a group of people she hid behind others. Eventually she pulled me aside, away from everyone, and whispered, 'How bad is it?'

I frowned. 'How bad is what?'

She let her face fall and her eyes roll, and then she aggressively pointed at her cheek. Behind the shadow of her fringe was a pimple, surrounded by a concealer shade that was slightly more orange than her pale, freckled skin.

I looked back at her worried eyes and laughed. 'It's literally fine. Like, it's a bit crusty but you can barely see it.'

She squinted her eyes suspiciously, but she lifted her head up a little, letting her hair fall back a bit and allowing more light to shine on her face. 'Are you sure? Should I put more concealer on?'

'Definitely not. Honestly I wouldn't have noticed it at all if you hadn't pointed it out. You still look like you, and you're still pretty.'

She grinned, and tucked her fringe behind her ear. Her little spot sat on her cheek, but her eyes gleamed. 'Okay good. Thank you!' And she floated away, back to the group of people who also couldn't give two shits about the clearness of her skin.

Turns out no one really cared about my skin either. The friends I had sleepovers with had insecurities of their own, and were most likely far too in their own heads about the way they thought I was looking at them to think about how I looked. And here's the thing: people might notice it, but is it going to affect the way they see you and treat you? I should absolutely hope not, and if it does, why on earth should you care about that person's opinion of you?

Now I can walk around barefaced in front of anyone, and I feel far more beautiful than I did as a teen with a secret layer of foundation on. There is something about confidence that is far more attractive than any physical quality, and even on the days where I feel just as gross as I did when I was younger, I push it away and pretend. 'Fake it till you make it' actually works. If you tell the world you're beautiful, it will believe you, and then you'll start believing it too.

* * *

Before you practise loving your spotty skin, you might as well look after it as best as you can.

1. Let's start internally. You'd be surprised at just how much my face changed entirely when I learned to drink more water and get enough sleep. I feel as though I usually fail at life targets when I really try them – I know, I'm the worst – so I accidentally achieved this by falling in love with green tea and not enjoying late night parties any more. I've always loved fruit and veggies and all things healthy, but my kryptonite was cheese. I used to buy a block and get through the whole thing within a week, pouring shredded cheddar over mountains of pasta, and then nibbling on cubes with grapes as snacks too. Dairy contains all sorts of hormones and I definitely recognised a connection to my breakouts, but life is short, and I fucking love cheese, so I cut down but definitely didn't cut out. But it was enough to help, and all these things combined absolutely helped to make my skin feel plumper and my face just look . . . awake. I wasn't walking around looking like a dehydrated zombie any more!

2. I'm going to say it – just in case you'll be able to take the advice that I can't seem to – but DON'T touch it. I've tried absolutely everything. In my little room in my old house, I wrote 'DON'T' in sharpie on my mirror, as if it would have been enough of a reminder to take my hands away from my face and stop me staring into my pores. I cut my nails short so it was harder to scratch, I asked my friends to tap me if they saw me picking, but even still, if there's a spot that's begging to be squeezed, I will.

So, if you can't stop like me, we can work around the problem. First, only touch your skin with clean hands, so as little bacteria as possible gets in. A warm face cloth will help to open up your pores, and ice cubes help tremendously with inflammation. If it doesn't burst (ew) then don't tug at it (also ew). If you're examining your face out of boredom, instead of wasting your time attacking your skin, use it to pamper. A face mask can help to heal and will also temporarily restrict your face from being prodded.

3. Learn from teenage me – drying out your face completely is not the answer. Your skin will just produce more oil in an attempt to rehydrate itself. Wash your face gently, and research and invest in some repairing oils.

4. For make-up, wear whatever you know will make you feel good, but also practise feeling good without those things. I used to completely paint over my skin because I couldn't bear the sight of any sort of redness or imperfection whatsoever. I posted a video showing my naked face up close, and someone told me that my scarring looked cute, like extreme freckles, so now I leave most of them to show in my daily make-up routine. I'll use a tinted moisturiser and some targeted concealer for the particularly angry bits, but I'm not afraid of letting them show any more.

MY FACE

Hello!
This is my skin.
Please mind your step on the pores, you might fall in.
Look it's purple, beneath your feet.
Yes, I'm only 20 – no, I don't get plenty of sleep.

Sometimes there are cheekbones
hidden under a smile,
and if you're really lucky
freckles pop up every once in a while.
I usually do a paint job
every single day,
so welcome
to my face.

Oh,
meet Mr Zit.
He's been around for so long, I'm starting to get used to it!
Let's swim through my brows;
they move so much they must have special powers.

Sometimes there are cheekbones
hidden under a smile,
and if you're really lucky
freckles pop up every once in a while.
I usually do a paint job
every single day,
so welcome
to my face.

I secretly like it here!
I secretly like it here.

PARTY TATTOOS

Take a look at the clock,
only so long to go,
scrubbing smooth young skin,
saying I don't know.
Grab a bag, grab a bottle,
but leave the what if –
you'll see it in the morning after your kicks.

All you will need for a rocking good time
is a bunch of people who don't give a damn!
There's a yes, in your head,
gotta find where it's at.
You'll lose it in the morning,
but ignore that.

We're not bruised,
they're just party tattoos!
And that colourful mess is just colourful regret.
Black lipstick will never be a sin.
We'll regret it when we're old, with wrinkled up skin.

My mummy said to always wear a coat;
but it's warm, and it's heavy, and we're trying to float!
Don't forget she'll be right when it's 3 a.m.,
so shiver, but shiver with a friend.

We're not bruised,
they're just party tattoos!
And that colourful mess is just colourful regret.
Black lipstick will never be a sin
We'll regret it when we're old, with wrinkled up skin.

Write a postcard to you at 84,
tell her you'd never dream of living behind a door.
Life was fun, full of love, full of hopeful smiles,
bet you wish you were here – but I'll see you in a while.

CHAMPAGNE AND CORNFLAKES

In 2015 I travelled around various places on tour. I've mentioned that I don't remember much of my Australian/New Zealand tour, but I came across this message that I'd sent to my friends describing something funny that had happened. It was meant to be just a short recap of the experience, but it ended up turning into a mini story. I wanted to add it in, because firstly this was a moment where I realised that I'd missed writing and I wanted to do more of it; and also to show just how dramatic I have always been. Dodie will always find some sort of meaning in everything. Enjoy!

I THINK I JUST HAD A FUCKING SPIRITUAL EXPERIENCE

I just tried to write it down but it turned into a story. Here is basically what happened in novel form. Some things may have been exaggerated but holy shit.

Okay so . . . I'm currently sitting in 74a, next to two guys, and I'm pretty sure the guy in 74b is reading this over my shoulder as I type.

I've just showered. I've de-tightsed but am wearing my slouchy massive stripy jumper dress, NO MAKE-UP, bad skin, bare legs and sandals. Oh, and short hair half tied up in a weird tiny ponytail. I have a cute fringe swoop going on tho.

And I'm trying to come to terms with what just happened.

I find a seat in the business lounge. I'm carrying my beige backpack, my PILLOW, and my uke. I ask for a champagne, set it down, and then because why the hell not, I get some cornflakes. It's free, it's breakfast, and I love cornflakes. I sit down, put them next to each other, and suddenly realise how stupid champagne and cornflakes look. I clearly do not belong in a business class lounge.

But you know what?! Fuck it. I'm going to own the weirdness. I decide to take a photo of my stupid naive breakfast.

I look up, to see who will be judging me.

Sitting opposite me, wearing a sky-blue shirt, tapping on his laptop, is the most stereotypical attractive man I have ever seen. He has thick brown hair, a jawline and cheekbones that could slice butter, and . . . Oh my. His sleeves are rolled up to reveal the most beautifully toned forearms I've ever seen.

I melt a little bit, fluff up my hair instinctively, and hold my phone above my dumb meal to take a photo.

I only get one, of course. I'm not drawing more attention to myself. It's not the best, but I can't deal with the pressure of the god sitting opposite me. I put my phone down on the glass table, pick up my silver spoon, and poke it around my cereal.

After a few minutes of a mixture of mushy milk and tangy booze, I hear a sigh, and the godly man sits upright in my peripheral vision. My stomach clenches.

'Enjoying your meal?'

I look up, and stare into a warm, kind, beautiful smile. 'I knew you were going to . . . like . . . notice this. I just thought it looked so stupid.' I grin at him, sipping my champagne as casually as I can. Another hair fluff. Not on purpose.

He grins back. 'What are you doing with the photo?'

His voice is deep, smooth and interesting. I can't place his accent. English? Australian? But the 'r' seemed so American and sharp.

Luckily I have a line ready in my head to say. It sounds cool. Casual. Comedic. 'I dunno. I might write a song. "champagne and cornflakes" sounds like an awesome band name.' I look down, stirring my spoon in the soggy orange lumps and smirking a little. He laughs back. Score!

'Are you sending it to a friend?'

'Maybe. I just wanted to capture the madness.'

'Brilliant. I just thought that it was the epitome of . . . The Jetlag Breakfast.'

'Well, there's something to wake up me up. And something to send me to sleep.'

'I was going to say . . . It'll help you nap. Are you coming or going?' He tilts his laptop screen down, smiling and squinting his eyes slightly, as if he's looking into a brighter light.

'I've just come from Melbourne. So, fourteen hours of sitting in the same spot, attempting to sleep upright. Eight more to go.'

'Ah, I'm going the other way. Just had my eight, now for the fourteen back home.'

As we chat back and forth, my head is squealing. How on earth is this painfully attractive man talking to a tired, skinny plain girl in a stripy oversized jumper? Am I smiling too much? Have I drunk this champagne too quickly?

We exchange the small talk basics. I manage to explain my YouTube, touring situation. He's into science, and does some presenting work with ABC. So, holy shit. No wonder he's so hot.

'So, I'm guessing you'll post that picture to Twitter?' He opens his laptop. 'Cause, you know, I'd like to follow your "champagne and cornflakes" release.'

'Haha. Sure. Um, yeah, it's . . . Doddleoddle. Stupid, I know. I chose it when I was like sixteen, and there's no going back now.'

'Gotcha. I feel you; turns out "Alan Cosmos" isn't actually as rare as you might think for a science geek. Oh yeah, Alan – that's me.'

'I'd never know. Hey, I'll follow you back.'

I click my phone on. Ah, shit. My gate's open. I should be boarding. 'Ah, I'd . . . I'd better be going. Got to get on a plane and all that.'

'Well.' He stretches, his broad shoulders widening. I have to consciously make an effort not to bite my lip. 'This was a wonderful five-minute chat. Thank you, and let me know how your new single goes.' He smirks.

'Nice chatting to you, Alan.' I smile back, my pitch ascending to nothing less than a squeak. I grab my uke, passport and fucking pillow, and sling my rucksack on my back, suddenly becoming painfully aware of what I look like.

'You too. Good luck! I have so much respect for beings who take risks to follow their dreams.'

I smile, give a final look, and walk away, enjoying the buzz of the champagne and dopamine in my brain, thanks to Alan Cosmos.

AFTER READING THIS BACK I JUST REALISED

IT'S A FUCKING METAPHOR

HE'S CHAMPAGNE

I'M CORNFLAKES

WHAT IS HAPPENINFHSB?

Confessions

A NON LOVE SONG

back, back,
it's time to go back to you know where;
but was it fun,
in the sun where you were?

stop, no –
no, you're not allowed to think that!
unwire the good,
don't imagine what could have been.
what a nice little holiday;
it's a memory now.

you fool,
how dare you trust fate! she's not that kind,
you stepped off the edge,
but you didn't check where you'd fall,
and now look at what you've done.
just a memory now.

shut it down,
get it into your brain –
this will all just end in flames!
where's that self-control that you preach?
and now look at what we've done;
just a memory now.

grief hurts, but it is still loving

WHAT'S IT LIKE?

Please be happy. When you are in a good mood, we feel like sunshine. There are no troubles, I don't feel any weight in my mind – I am tied to hundreds of helium balloons that let me leap and land softly with every step. Everything is so easy and beautiful; effortless laughter, pure, gooey delight.

I want you to be as close to me as possible, at every minute of the day. When we pull away, all I can think about is coming closer again. My heart glows in my centre, bright, white, yellow, pink, orange, deep reds and purples.

Feeling cared for by the human who does this to me is the closet thing to magic I will ever experience. I am so grateful, so lucky to have you look into my eyes and wish them to be happy. Can I really make your chest feel like mine?

November 28th 2009

Gah, I havent written in so long. Im just too
busy nowadays - Year 10 is So Hard. Ok, lets
fill in. I had an operation - which I hated. Ok,
being in a cosy bed eating chocolate the whole
day wasnt so bad, but the anesthetic was
horrible.
Granny is alive, but wobbely. She told me not to
be sad when she dies. But of course I will be.
I keep getting ill. Taking so many pills.

20th Feb 2011 :-) :-)

I really really really want a boyfriend. Someone
who loves me for who I am, and all the crazy
thing I do, someone who is gorgeous, with GREAT
hair, and a cute face. Tally kind of skinny, pale,
funny, kind - someone who I would feel
comfortable/brilliant kissing. I want to kiss
a guy like that. But where are they all???
People keep saying I am pretty. I hope that is
true, and they arent just saying it to be nice.
Bye x x x

CRUSH

You'll have to excuse my fourteen-year-old brain. I did a little research on my old Facebook conversations and I dug deep into my 2009 memory banks. What's hilarious is that I remember thinking I had learned all that I'd ever learn, and that everyone around me just didn't understand what I was going through when they were trying to give me advice. I felt truly unlovable, from myself and anyone I fancied:

* * *

Omg. I love him. Every time I look at the corner of the room I imagine us both rolling around on the floor. He is SOOO FITTTTT.

First of all, you are fourteen; hold off a little. Also, that's not as exciting as you think it is. Second, that's not love. You don't even know him. Like, actually know him. I know you'll argue that you do, but people are not what they seem on the surface – ESPECIALLY at fourteen.

I DO KNOW HIM. Anyway, I can get to know him. If I wear my Uggs and leggings and that long top with my padded bra and lip gloss and fluff up my hair a bit I bet he'd notice me. I can imagine him looking at me like 'wow'.

Oh, Dodie. There is absolutely some boy on this earth at your time who would love even the things you hate; which I know, at this age, is a lot. They'd find your bracey smile cute, your extreme excitement at everything endearing, your poker-straight badly layered hair as stylish. But this particular boy will never look at you the way you want to be looked at, no matter how willing you are to mould yourself into whatever he would find attractive. The more you pour your thoughts into obsessing over what you're not, the more you're going to hate yourself.

That's what all the magazines say: learn to love yourself. But I hate my nose and my non-existent boobs and my spots and my hands and feet and arms and EVERYTHING. I will never love myself :(

All right, Miss Dramatic. But yes, sorry – you're insecure. And it will take years of experimentation with make-up, dress sense and even different mannerisms before you settle into someone you're happy being. You will get there; but for the next three years or so you're going to seek affirmation from people who don't know you and certainly don't love you because you're the most terrified of what they think of you. And honestly this is something you'll still struggle with now and again in your twenties; but soon you will learn that those people's opinions don't matter at all. It would be good if you could pour all your efforts into being the best person you can be for the people who do know you, not the coolest person for the ones who don't, but you will learn these lessons messily; and sometimes that's the best way. Also, here's a curveball; you could potentially talk to this guy and actually tell him that you like him, rather than taking sneaky photos of him and trying to get his attention by telling terrible jokes.

WHAT?! No! Are you crazy? That would end in flames! He would never talk to me again!

Ah yes, I bet you'd miss those many long, deep conversations you've both shared together. What was it last week? Didn't he ask you for one of your prawn cocktail crisps?

I'm being mean. What I'm trying to say is, if even the idea of being honest to someone is enough to send you into a panic about a lack of contact, perhaps this isn't someone you should be spending so much time thinking about. Furthermore, if someone doesn't want to know you, why on earth would you want to know them?

Point is, you're gonna be okay. You will daydream and obsess over this boy who is not right for you in any way, and in a few years' time you will be asked out on a date by someone you wouldn't expect to want to know. But he will look at you the way you have been waiting to be looked at, and the way you will learn to look at yourself.

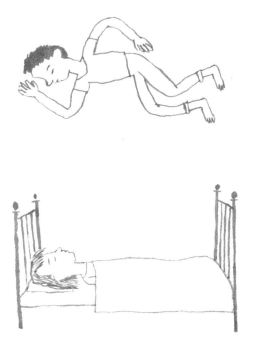

AN AWKWARD DUET

Do you want to go first?
'Cause I'm happy to wait –
I practised really hard,
but I'm finding it strange to start
with you.

So how does it go?
I've forgotten the tune, I
haven't warmed up today,
so I might sound a bit strange;
(yes, I do).

And I can sing!
I swear it's true;
I'm just a little nervous in front of you.

So who's on the 3rd?
I think I'm better at melody!
Oh, I'm going to get it wrong,
shall we try another song?
No? . . . okay.

Let's just go for a take!
And see how we sound!
(My heart is beating fast,
oh, vocal cords please last!)
Here we go!

'Cause I can sing!
I swear it's true;
I'm just a little nervous in front of you.

* * *

I think I messed up,
I just wanted to improvise.
Shall we do this another day?

. . . well . . . I think I sounded great.

And I can sing!
I swear it's true;
I'm just a little nervous in front of you.

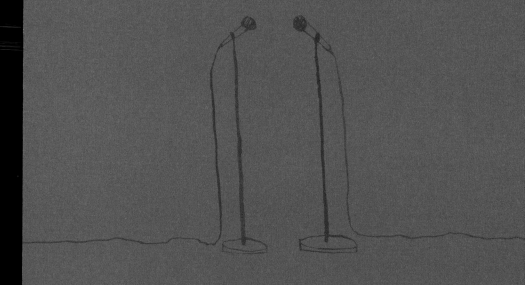

AWKWARD

The most awkward day of my life was in 2010 on my first date. A boy in my theatre group who I'd chatted to and flirted with a bit (well – I didn't really know how to flirt at fifteen – there was a lot of hair fluffing and loud giggling) had strolled up to me after rehearsal and asked me out. I squeaked out an 'okay!' and then continued to panic for the days leading up to our planned day of ice skating and pizza. Alice had then warned me that I should never go on a dinner date with a boy ('he can't watch you EAT, you're a fucking mess when you consume food') so I cancelled the pizza. Turns out the ice skating session had to be pre-booked, so we didn't end up doing that either. I wore my favourite woollen booties, SOAKED myself in Claire's Accessories perfume, and practically emptied an entire can of hairspray on my backcombed hair. Mum dropped me off in the shopping centre and I wandered up to a boy in a grey coat, who also reeked of product. We greeted each other with shaky voices and hugged quickly, misjudging which side either of us would lean to and ending up in a sort of cheek-to-cheek collision of bodies. That moment set the bar on where the awkwardness level would be for the rest of the day, and so we shuffled around Harvey Harlow Centre in the most painful, cringe-filled silence.

We both frantically searched for a way to make conversation, but every topic thrown out there by either one of us for some reason was closed up in less than five sentences.

'Do you want to get some chocolate from the sweet shop?'

'I don't really like chocolate really. I might get some fizzy strawbs though.'

'Oh really? How can you not like chocolate?'

'I don't know.'

'Oh. Okay.'

And then it would return back to the nausea-inducing atmosphere and I'd wonder how on earth I could leave as soon as possible. I think I'd even planned out a way to set up a fake fainting episode, and I was a just a few painful sentences away from dropping to the floor as a way to escape.

Somehow the day ended, and I vowed to never ever spend a day with just one other person whom I didn't know very well again.

Two things I was sure would be certain from that day:

1. Some people were just good at being social, and I was not one of those people. One-on-one interactions had a massive black X over them, and I would forever cling to people I knew well in unfamiliar situations.

2. I would never talk to that boy again.

Turns out I was wrong about both. One-on-one interactions, especially with people you don't know, have a special sort of intimacy I now live for. At first, it might be like a game; you're both dancing your way through sentences, trying to land on something solid to lay a conversation on. And sometimes you won't; but the silence doesn't have to be uncomfortable. I will smile through it, and then open myself up. I am not afraid of being vulnerable, because it encourages others to be too, and then there's no games, or dancing; just pure, excited connection.

(Of course I don't have the complete hang of this; no one does! I still have terrible social experiences, and I'll go for weeks obsessing about something I said that didn't land as planned. But I like to keep the idea of it positive, and I'll keep practising and enjoying my one-on-one chatter.)

And that boy ended up being my first kiss and one of my best friends throughout secondary school. Turns out a terrible hello or a terrible goodbye might take a few times to get right.

BEN'S VIEW OF MY CONCERT

I'm the guy Dodie snogged in school.

Mid-morning Dodie texted me out of nowhere. She was putting a gig on tonight and wondered if I was around to pop down. She sent over the time and place.

I hadn't seen Dodie all year and I wanted to catch up with her.

When I walked in, the bar was empty. Wooden panelling for miles. Barman a bit tinny. Not a concert to be found.

'I'm here!' I messaged her. I'm not convinced.

I tried to find the toilet. It was invisible to the naked eye – surprise, it's one of the wooden panels – but before I could enter I received a reply: 'Give ur name at the door!'

I spied the side-door back towards the entrance and headed down a dark set of stairs. The gig was rammed. Across the crowd, and past a set of spacious booths, a band wearing denim smacked out something rhythmic. I had that weird feeling I've started having in certain situations recently: I'm possibly the oldest person in the room.

At this point I realised that I didn't have any more information about what the plans were. I wished that one of us had spelled it out. I'd assumed I would stride up to some sort of backstage and approach a stern bouncer. He would demand my name; I would provide it; he would pause for effect, then permit me to enter, and his severe demeanour would transform into a fatherly pride.

But it was not to be! All I could see of a backstage was a tiny door directly behind the band, and climbing across their cramped performance would have looked rude.

'I'm guessing I won't see you beforehand so break a leg!' I messaged her. To my right there was a merch table tucked away from the crowd. Behind it I recognised Dodie's mum. When she spotted me she reached across and gave me a big hug.

The last time we'd made eye contact, I'd called Dodie up at 11 p.m., professing my love through drunken sobs, so her welcoming gesture was a pleasant surprise.

Dodie responded: 'Yeah I'm just chillin in a booth!'

As you can see, the music was so loud we had to shout in our texts.

'Chill away my dear!' I replied.

'Come say HI!'

I craned my head. Neon-lit booths of beautiful youths tapped their phones to the tempo of the songs and ran wine-slick fingers through their hair.

To the side of 'the glamorous' I spotted Dodie in a booth with some friends. I squeezed through the people throwing her polite but wondering glances and at last wedged in among her and her friends. Finally the evening plans made sense, and I felt like I'd come across as awkward and silly.

'I was directing a play called 5 Lesbians Eating a Quiche . . .'

The girl next to me lost it.

'What? It's a great title.'

'No, I love it.'

'And why did it go wrong?' another guy asked.

'Oh, we had problems with patents, some of the actors were flaky . . . But we received several five-star reviews.'

'Ideal! One for each lesbian,' he replied.

Dodie and I had a quick catch-up in each other's ears. Our lives were iffy, three out of five stars. That's all we managed to catch up between us. Before long we were all gently heckling the Brummy band.

Later on, Dodie said something I've heard her say a few times before on similar occasions. 'It's so weird watching you all together. It's like these different worlds colliding!' She squirmed and laughed at the same time, as if watching a magic trick.

By now she probably qualifies as famous: hardly a household name, but enough to be recognised in public, or to appear on the side of buses. Dodie has a significant community of fans supporting her work. I wonder how much this lady who has carved a successful career in the music industry still feels tethered to the sixteen-year-old I was friends with?

I realised what the evening was about. Our friends were a way for us to draw ourselves tighter. Inviting us there that night, she had reassembled these distant parts of herself, stacked them against each other, and at last could laugh at the beautiful shape they made. Herself reflected back at her – something comforting, something reassuring.

The band finished playing and Dodie was called onto the stage. We wolf-whistled and over-cheered and she shushed us, embarrassed. It was a game: could we get her to break her stubborn humility?

For a moment it felt like we were winning – she was growing embarrassed – until a change came over her, and she couldn't hear us. She was focusing. She pottered onto the stage – then she conquered it. For the next half hour she was untouchable.

'Fuck. I love eighteen plus gigs. It's like you're my people.'

And the crowd loved it.

Vanessa Place wrote that everything can be art; the task of the artist is just to work out how you can put something so that it becomes art. In Dodie's performance she's worked out how to put herself on the stage. This is really what seems to be the centre of her appeal. Over time she has built her courage, revealing her secrets, her insecurities, guilts, trials. She has since become an artist, honoured with putting into words what many cannot, revealing experiences many had not recognised, and then making them sing.

And what impresses me the most now is that Dodie has become a powerful lyricist. Every word is made to count, they glow beneath the music. It's a sign that her talent is evolving: there's a career ahead of her.

It's a privilege to be inspired by a friend, and I've found it's a rare one.

Dodie plays '6/10', a song about insecurity – recognisably hers from school. But I also notice that it's not confessional; she isn't just telling a story. Take this line: 'Oh, I'll just call a taxi/I've gotta be up early tomorrow again.'

It feels like such an obvious thing for anyone to say at the end of a shitty evening. Notice that it's an excuse to leave. It's a feeble, empty saying, one we recognise as hiding any number of agonies. The feeling that you're wasting your time – specifically, all of it. The feeling that the night hasn't gone on for long enough; with just a little more time, it could have turned perfect. And the feeling that the night has gone on for too long. Not everyone can produce a line as subtle as this. Everyone's trying to.

Dodie succeeds in creating beautiful songs because she isn't scared of being afraid. The difference between a song that speaks to you and a song that you cringe at is that the success expresses vulnerability without fear.

And how is that? Dodie's bravery comes from her comfort with living honestly. She's in the business of sharing everything dear to her, sooner or later. In realising that, and being true to herself, nothing can touch her. This has only come from years of practice; she has had to earn it, but its importance has mattered beyond her art. Mastery of a craft is also the discovery of how best to make oneself.

I remember once when she came to visit me while I was finishing my degree and we were discussing how we'd spent the past few years.

'But anyone can do it,' she insisted, referring to her YouTube channel. 'Everyone should do it. Buy yourself a camera and just talk.' Everyone had the potential. It was something I had always believed, but Dodie knew it, she was adamant. I asked her at what point her hobby became her profession.

'I don't understand why it happened. I kinda got lucky on a few occasions, which opened up several doors. But considering how lazy I am, seriously, anyone can do it.'

Though she said this at the time with her familiar humility, we both knew she hadn't been lazy. We all have that weird habit of saying that, don't we? Only last week I called her and said the same thing. She was quick to correct me, and spoke in a measured, methodical way:

'Everyone has lazy periods and productive periods. You'll pick it up more intensely soon.'

We live for long enough to fall in love with thousands of artists, valuing them all uniquely – so, yes, anyone can do it. There is enough room in the world for your creation too, and you don't need to be famous. With a platform like YouTube, a small audience can mean enough.

Between songs Dodie chatted with the audience. Interestingly I found Dodie talked more confidently on stage than she ever did in person. Granted, it's less awkward to say personal things to a room than to talk about them. But the audience is her best friend: someone who understands her; who makes her laugh and finds her funny; who she would give anything to. She introduced a new song she'd just finished writing, 'Would You Be So Kind', and it was about a guy she had been seeing and had fallen in love with.

'Well, after I finished the song, it got all messy, which is classic . . . So now the song doesn't really work. Anyhow. Fuck it!'

'Fuck it!' the audience concurred.

I wonder what it's like for her to repeat tricky experiences in concerts, to replay them. Week after week she has to dive back into that place in her mind. The professional can't forget or begin to heal over the difficult things; she must carry them with her from gig to gig. Performing must be exhausting.

A friend of mine once showed me a tattoo on his forearm. It was of an ex-lover's signature.

'Yeah, the relationship went sour,' he said, 'but the tattoo isn't a regret because it's a reminder of exactly when I got it, when things were at their best. Life changed. But that moment, that little while, didn't.'

What he later found, what was surprising, was that he started to feel that his tattoos changed with him. Though the moment it represented couldn't be altered, its legacy was constantly evolving. It aged with him; the bond with his memory, its beauty and pain, grew kinder, forgiving, the way friendships do.

It's hard seeing a friend under emotional pressure. Fame comes with a lot of difficulties and pressures. She's doing something incredible with her life, but at the end of the day I hope my friend is okay. It's clear that the only way Dodie will thrive and be happy is by going forward. So I'm left with this tension, hoping that she keeps going and going – and that as the pressures rise she can rise with them. Which, of course, she will.

We love her, her friends, her fans, but that's a lot of love to bear.

Connecting to people on the most fundamental levels brings with it an unexpected responsibility. People share their problems with Dodie because that's human nature: when someone gives you a part of themselves, you feel safe enough to share something back with them.

And, of course, any human being in that position wants to help. You would do your best to reply to those people.

But then one day, years ago, when I visited her flat, Dodie opened a cupboard in her kitchen. It was full of fan mail. Quite literally, rammed. Picture it, really: the average letter or card is, what, a few millimetres thick, ten centimetres wide? And her cupboard was probably a metre deep, thirty centimetres wide. Hundreds of people – several hundred – had reached out to Dodie, and were waiting for a reply.

'I want to read all of it, but I can't always reply to everything. That's the hardest thing. Sometimes you're too late, and there's never enough time . . . Or sometimes people try to take advantage of you. I can't help everyone directly when they share their problems with me, and that's really difficult. But I'm not a trained therapist. It's not safe for me or them to help like that. So I can't help in that way. All I can do is keep creating. And that's so hard.'

Benjamin Redwood
London
26 September 2016

INTERTWINED

Skin
Heat
Hair in your mouth
Feet touching feet

Oh, you
and I
safe from the world
though the world will try –

Oh, I'm afraid of the things in my brain
but we can stay here
and laugh away the fear

Numb
Fine
You create a rarity of my genuine smiles

So breathe,
breathe with me
Can you drink all my thoughts?
'Cause I can't stand them!

Intertwined
Free
I've pinned each and every hope on you
I hope that you don't bleed with me

I'm afraid of the things in my brain
But we can stay here
And laugh away the fear

MEN I HAVE LOVED

He is angry. He is judgemental. He is arrogant. He is selfish. He is overbearing, solid and warm bodied. He squints his eyes and heaves out pointed sighs that make my throat close up and my torso tense and my heart race and my eyes leak. The highs aren't that high, and they are so fragile, like thin ice. The lows are frequent, panic-inducing, horrible. The middle of the two is confusion; familiar confusion.

He is soft. He is warm, like a laid-in quilt or pillow. He is hilarious and bright and so interesting. He runs and jumps and moves his eyebrows and stretches into straight-teethed grins that fill me with safety. His lungs buzz, and the music sprints up his throat to be chewed into hundreds of syllables that dance around the room. I know that he will be with me forever and I must never lose him. He is my rock.

He is quiet. He is colder. He is mathematical, complex, intelligent. For some reason, our bodies fit well together, like two pieces of wood that slot in perfectly. My eyes flicker up and down him and my mouth waters at the idea of holding his strong jaw in my hand, inhaling his air, tasting his soul; maybe because it reminds me that he is not just machinery on the inside. Like me, though, he is broken.

YOU

I told you I was looking for some empathy.
Well, you fooled me
Just a touch and a thought and I was gone,
And now someone's gonna get to know the better you.
When I was supposed to?
Oh, why did it have to be you?

I guess
now the next time there's an opportunity
I'll tread more carefully.
My heart's running out of Sellotape!
You know
how is it I've never felt that way before?
I was so sure
it wasn't going to be you!

Why do all the red flags
just look like so much fun?
I have a habit of
searching for the damage
to share my love

I promised to be numb,
but somehow you were the one.
Now to unwind
months of a good time.

People will tell me that I messed up,
and it wasn't love,
and I'm secretly hoping they are right; because
whatever it was it was wonderful –
but non-functional.
Oh,

I really hope I don't love you.

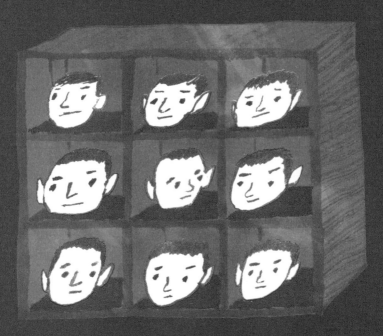

Dodie.

HOW.

Your are FUCK UGLY

he is BEAUTIFUL.

your face

LOLLL

actually
loling ut
yourself.

his

♡ AYAY

AY

I haven't met him
yet. But I love him.
I don't even know.
I am a little scared.
This could be big.
I ♡ his songs. ──▷ pb

MY MANIPULATIVE, UNHEALTHY RELATIONSHIP

I had just turned seventeen, and I was awkward, skinny and weird. I had a best friend called Alice, and we would make twisted faces across the room and burst into ugly laughter. She'd do my make-up and we'd laugh at how big my nose could look in pictures and we'd film ourselves roly-polying across the floor and end up in a heap of giggles. We'd gossip over boys in our school and cringe at bad kisses at parties where we hadn't learned how to drink responsibly yet; and then freak out when they'd text and help craft replies of rejection.

I'd had a couple of boyfriends – one was a boy friend/boyfriend, who was incredibly sweet and I shared my first kiss with, but I mostly liked just for company. The other was fairly long distance (for someone who was still in school) and it was exciting, but overall he didn't care and it wasn't serious at all. It was looking like I was on track to my and Alice's pact to marry at thirty; all boys were immature and all the fit ones would never be interested in us.

He was twenty-two. He wrote me long, in-depth letters about music, adventures, love. He was a surfer, had the flicky hair Alice and I would swoon over, and would go rock climbing and running – so he definitely had a six-pack. We had four-hour-long phone calls and we'd text at least every half hour, taking it in turns to ask each other questions like 'What would you spend a million pounds on? Who's the most famous person you've met? If you could only have one meal for the rest of your life what would it be?'

When we met for the first time, he ran off his train, bounded through the barriers and scooped me up in his ginormous arms, lifting me and twirling me round the station. I was a little embarrassed but I didn't care. Look! Look at this man! This man fancies me.

I had a mammoth spot on my chin and a terrible cold, and although he kept his distance because he didn't want to get ill he still called me the next day. And the day after that, and the day after that.

He moved to London and I'd get the train in after sixth form to visit his flat, finding him waiting for me at my platform grinning and holding pink flowers. He asked me to please not talk about exams so much around his flatmates? If I had to, maybe call it college, or something. I understood. He also asked me to wipe my socks before I got on his bed so I didn't bring all the fluff onto his covers, and spit my toothpaste into the running water so it didn't stick to the sink. He tutted but laughed at my terrible sense of direction on our walks to the shops, holding my hand and leading the way, or the way I'd chop onions haphazardly because no one had taught me how yet, grabbing the chopping board and instructing me to watch and learn. I'd started to feel a little incompetent and stupid; I didn't know why I forgot things, or couldn't do things as well as he did, but also I didn't know why it mattered so much. He'd make popcorn and pour me red wine and we'd snuggle up on the sofa, tickling each other's arms and sitting in electric excitement while we watched movies, until it was time for me to travel home for school the next day.

I finished my A levels in the summer and so I started staying round his and spending more days together. About four months in, I was washing up after an evening of pasta and wine. He had asked me if I could help out around the flat a little bit more, so I was trying to show him that I cared. I can't remember if he was frustrated about something before, or if this really did come out of nowhere, but he grabbed a bowl I'd placed upturned on the side and slammed it upside down on the counter dramatically. I jumped and stared at him, terrified. He stared back, his eyes angry and wide, the clang of the bowl ringing through the silence.

So I didn't know how to drain a bowl when washing up. I mumbled an apology and we got ready for bed without a saying a word to each other, my heart pounding and my head spinning. Did that really happen? Who was this man?

I can't remember exactly how the shouting started. He was angry that I was so lazy – too lazy to care, to try, to think, and he felt as though he was running around me, picking up everything I failed at doing. It somehow started to make sense to me, and I felt awful; of course he was so upset when I was so incompetent. I burst into tears and apologised, saying sorry for every point he'd made. He hugged me and I melted, relieved and desperate to get back to how we were before. I definitely wasn't in the mood to have sex, but I wanted to be on his side again, and there was no way I could have said no now. He finished, and we curled up in the dark.

'So what are you going to work on from now on?' he said. I panicked. I needed to get this right.

'Showing you that I care by not being lazy.' It worked. He kissed the back of my neck, and whispered 'thank you'. And so we went back to happier, snuggly us, for a while; but with all bowls drained properly, and all onions cut neatly.

I would tiptoe around him, saying and doing all the right things, and we would be so good together. He'd tell me I was 'his', and he'd hold my hand at events proudly, taking every opportunity to boast to the room that this was true. I'd bat his hands away playfully, uncomfortable at the public display but happy I was loved. At one particular party I noticed a friend I hadn't seen in a long time in the corner of the room. I slipped my hand out of my boyfriend's and bounded across the room, wrapping my arms around him. We caught up excitedly, gushing about the months we'd missed. 'Oh! And my boyfriend's just over there.' I turned around, ready to point him out, but I couldn't spot him. I turned back, apologised, and we continued to gossip about our lives.

The silence lasted the whole way home. I'd try to hold his hand, but it would be limp, so I'd pull it back and hug my arms. I'd gather enough courage to ask him how his night was, and he'd shrug softly, looking away. On our walk back from the station, he finally spoke.

'How was Luke?'

My heart sank. Oh.

I had left him; I had utterly abandoned him at a party where he didn't know too many people, and why couldn't we have gone up to Luke together? Luke clearly fancied me, we could have said hello as a team, but instead I ran off without thinking, or caring, as usual. But I had looked for him afterwards, I said! I was excited to show him off too – well, all he saw was me running towards another boy and being all over him; how embarrassing for the whole room of people to see. I said sorry, but just sorry wasn't enough this time, and so we were there again; up until the early hours of the morning, me desperately trying to make it all okay again, frantically searching for the right apology. I'd find it eventually, but this would be marked down as Another Act of a Lack of Care from Dodie, threatening the happy days with a possibility to be reopened for another evening of shouting.

I understood abusive relationships as physical. I told a few people about the way he'd throw things around and kick walls when he was shouting at me, and they'd say 'well, all right, but if he ever lays a finger on you, let me know'. And I know that he never would; and so it must have been okay. He'd take my phone and write messages to my flatmate in my name, crafting it with me to let her know that his bellowing last night was 'just a little tiff, we both made some mistakes but we're all better now', after she told me she was close to calling the police after hearing my sobs. But surely it wasn't abuse if I loved him? I felt terrible that people might not understand that he was angry because I had done something wrong. Like he said, anger was just an emotion, and he was perfectly within his right to feel and express his emotions, just like I did with my crying. Besides, his flowers were never an apology gift, because he never had to say sorry.

After two years of walking on eggshells and multiple failed attempts of me breaking up with him (they were the only times he would cry instead of shout), I was moving away from the town we'd both been living in for the last six months. My tenancy agreement had run out and I had lost my shop job, and it was pretty clear that I wasn't making any attempts to look for replacements nearby. He packed out the removal van he had helped me to hire, brushed the hair out of my streaming eyes and kissed me goodbye. I felt as though part of me was being torn away, and it hurt so much; but there was something strong, rooted deeply within me, that told me this was right.

I was so overwhelmed by the kindness of my London friends. I'd go with them to a party and stay stuck to them the whole night, constantly asking if they were okay and if they needed anything from me. They'd grab my arms and smile into me: 'Dodie! I'm okay! Really! Just go and enjoy yourself.'

If there was a silence in the room when we'd be hanging out, panic would settle in and I'd swallow a little harder. Tears would prickle my eyes and I'd wait for the heavy sighs while skimming over the past sentences in my head to try and work out what I'd said wrong. I'd be about to apologise, and suddenly they'd chuckle at something they'd read online, or ask me if I wanted a cup of tea, and I'd squeak a reply far too quickly, desperately trying not to breathe out my obvious relief too shakily.

My experience of a manipulative relationship helped me to understand that they are not as black and white as I first thought. Despite the warning signs matching up to what I was going through, I didn't see how it could have been abuse if it came from someone who loved me so much, and who I loved back. But it can, and it was. Not drinking enough water in the day, having too much cheese on your pasta and draining dishes the wrong way does not warrant an evening of shouting. You should be allowed to make your own choices in your life about how much you exercise, the friends you keep and the way you look, without being made to feel guilty. Sex should never be an apology and you should never be made to feel guilty for not giving it, and if anger is a common emotion from them then there is something wrong. Mistakes and wrongdoings will be present in every relationship, but the way to deal with them is through communication, empathy and love. No one is ever 100% right all the time, and if you are with someone who cannot admit that, then you will find yourself taking on all the blame, and it will slowly destroy you.

Put your energy into the relationships that make you feel good and build you up, not those that knock you down. True love and care with someone does not look like cold shoulders in an entire evening of apologies, or shouting at someone sobbing in the corner of a room, and although I can't go back to tell myself these things,

I'm hopefully able to tell someone else with a new rule book in their head given to them by someone who tends to get angry.

PAS DE DEUX

Poppy's a dancer
just turned sixteen
stares at boys who wear glasses
in Look magazine.

Here comes Tommy,
with glasses and all,
flowers in hand and ambitious plans,
it's not hard to fall.

She's walking on rivers,
he lifts her above,
she's full of belonging,
and so full of love.

Things get a bit louder,
Tommy's focused on plans,
his smile's replaced with an aggressive face;
but she'll still hold his hand.

Now she's given up dancing,
Tommy says she's too old.
He says focus on me, but she disagrees
while she does as she's told

Are you walking on eggshells?
And when push comes to shove
are you full of belonging
but not full of love?

Back to the studio
where she was told not to go,
feeling sick with guilt, the tension builds
as she opens the door.
And what else would be there
but a trusting pair
of strong bodies, lacking in worries, performing a pas de deux.

I am not right,
yes, this is what's right!
Souls, and hearts and minds intertwined!
No, I won't be defined by him any more.

She was walking on eggshells
and when push came to shove,
she was full of belonging
but not full of love.

So goodbye to Tommy,
And hello to Sam.
He doesn't wear glasses, but he loves how she dances,
and he'll hold her hand.

Yes, Poppy's a dancer,
with plans of her own.
You'll see her and partner
performing a pas de deux
in the old studio.

She's walking on rivers,
he lifts her above,
they're full of belonging
and so full of love.

I DIDN'T LIKE SEX

Before I became sexually active, I thought sex was like porn. One of my early boyfriends seemed to think that too, and so most of the sex I had in my first two years was uncomfortable, embarrassing and scary. I knew that I wasn't someone who should hate it – I'd daydream about it, I'd crave it, I wanted it. But the moment the real opportunity was there, I'd honestly start to feel sick. I couldn't stand the idea of myself . . . like that. I was made to feel like it wasn't okay to say no, that if I didn't want to do something it was because I didn't 'care enough to try', and honestly that I wasn't very 'good'. When I was made to feel bad at it, me and the little self-confidence I had shrank under the bed sheets. I longed for a hug that wasn't a demand for the thing that immediately filled me with shame.

There's a lot of pressure for women to be 'good in bed' – I was absolutely brought up in a world where our worth was in sex. I felt I was a failure at being a female, and I was so upset and disappointed that the thing I'd dreamed of and romanticised in my head was actually unbearable. I'd close my eyes and hug him tightly through it, and then I'd slip away to cry in the bathroom. I was convinced I'd hate it forever, and I'd be doomed to a life of discomfort and pressure.

I had two years of that. It was kind of like dancing – sober, self-conscious, awkward, pressured dancing – and it was pretty shit.

Then I started seeing someone else, and they'd ask me if I was okay and tell me I was wonderful. It still took a while until I could see my body sexually, but every now and again I'd peek and marvel at myself.

I wasn't made to feel guilty for the times I couldn't look, or even for the times I wanted to just cuddle and sleep.

Now, it's like music.

I melt away and I mostly don't even notice my body. I can look at myself in my underwear and know that I should be worshipped in sex.

So, it turns out sex is mostly nothing like porn – porn is based on straight, testosterone-fuelled male fantasies, and while there's nothing wrong with a little bit of that now and again, the idea that porn is the textbook guide for what real sex is like is absolutely ridiculous and incredibly damaging for newbies like I was.

Real sex is usually messy, awkward and hilarious, and I wish I'd known that before I started.

HOW TO HAVE SEX

A guide from a slightly self-conscious twenty-two-year-old woman who has had an average amount of experience. Although I am bisexual, the majority of sex I've had has been with a man, so this is based around that. (Also, sexual experiences are different for everyone. But I wanted to try to portray a realistic depiction of sexual intimacy, because sex is ultimately meant to be a fun and human thing for enjoyment. It just usually goes a bit like this. Also, this is a little embarrassing. I can't believe I'm putting this in a book. Oh well!)

* * *

You will need:

* initial vocal consent from both/all participants

* possible towel laid underneath bodies in case of any kind of spillages

* toilet roll for clean up (alternatives include towel mentioned earlier, or specific unloved T-shirt from laundry bin)

* a loo nearby to wee before and after (and sometimes in a break in the middle), especially for vagina owners. Tap for washing hands and . . . other areas . . . also comes in handy

* full glasses of water placed nearby (kissing and gasping dries out mouths like you wouldn't believe)

* hairband (especially if you have long hair and are on top)

* if penises are involved, an easily accessible condom or two, and/or other contraception. Also sexual health check-ups and trust

STEP 1 – SHALL WE?

The idea for sexual activity usually arises in the air after a long period of kissing, or spooning. First and foremost, gain that consent mentioned before. This is usually as simple as 'do you want to?' and a certain positive reply, like 'yes'. Also, gain consent from yourself – ask your body and brain if you want it. If you're uncertain, and confused on how to say so, then say something like 'I don't know' or 'I'm not too sure'. You should pause and talk it through and reach a healthy decision. Sex should be a fun activity for all participants.

STEP 2 – ROLLING AROUND

After mutual agreement, there's usually a section of various types of foreplay. This can include:

* fumbling around the lower areas (it took me a while to find a penis in my first experiences, which should have been hilarious if it wasn't for the unhealthy relationship I was in)

* fun and experimental making out, with lip biting and mouth exploring. You'll find some techniques to be a hit, and others . . . not so much. (Hits and misses usually change with different partners)

* touching, grabbing and oral things, the latter probably a bit strange and scary at first

Communication is the key, and you can still be sexy and ask things (do you like that?/tell me what you want).

Excitement levels rise and it's easy to get lost in feeling.

STEP 3 – HERE WE GO

Once you're both ready, there might be a break in contact of reaching for the condom. A tip to make this seemingly long moment less awkward is to smile and laugh along. Note: remember that it's always okay to change your mind at any point. If you suddenly feel uncomfortable, you can say something like 'hold up', 'wait', or 'hang on a second, I'm not feeling too great'.

If penetration is involved, make sure there's lots of lubrication. Spit is probably the easiest if you're unprepared, but use actual lube for best results. If it's your first time, take it super slow – it might be a little uncomfortable.

Another note: 'popping your cherry' is actually a fake concept. There's no seal of skin that bursts like a pen through a piece of paper (the idea of that literally makes me feel ill) – the hymen is just stretchy skin that surrounds the vaginal opening. Vaginas aren't like unpopped jam jars – they can be stretched open in other ways.

STEP 4 – THE MAIN EVENT

Sex is a lot of limbs, giggles and manoeuvring bodies. It can be intimate and romantic in places, but you will struggle to find one person who's never dealt with an elbow in the face or a fanny fart. There shouldn't be judgement, pressure or discomfort; the whole point is that it's meant to be enjoyable. Sometimes there are orgasms, sometimes there are slip-ups (or slip-outs, am I right? Eyyyy), and sometimes the whole thing is just not right, and you have to have a break, but it's okay. You should never be made to feel embarrassed about something so personal, especially when you're in the most vulnerable state you can be. Keep communicating, keep relaxed, and enjoy it.

STEP 5 – GO TO THE TOILET

Films tend to skip out the super romantic and graceful 'toilet visit' after sex. Or if they don't, then they skip out the days of painful peeing from infections and weeks of antibiotics from the doctor. Give yourself a little bit of spooning time, but make sure you have a wee (and a wash, if you can) after sex. It'll also give you an opportunity to check how badly smudged your eyeliner is, to fix that bed hair and have a little freshen up. Then you can tiptoe back to bed for UTI-free snuggling and more communication. Ask questions! And say what was good, and whatever wasn't, say how it could be good (I'd be mortified at criticism; positive encouragement is much better).

Sex education in my school was a video of swimmers racing in their little hats, a picture slideshow of scary rashes, and a leaflet on where to get the morning after pill. I should have known that it was okay to say no to sex, whatever the circumstances, and I should have known that if I wasn't having fun, then I shouldn't be participating.

I also could have done with the 'make sure you pee after sex' information. That would have saved me from countless terrible experiences.

HUMAN

This is about getting to know someone you are fascinated by. I'd spent a lot of time with someone who I wanted to know more about. There was a spark, and I was excited to open up and explore who I was and who he was together. I wanted to be absorbed and absorb; I wanted to sit on the floor and drink and share with this person, because I had so much to say and I was so excited. I didn't know what it was, but the only label it needed was that it was 'human'. We were two complex people with incredible souls who wanted to be in each other's company. And it was wonderful.

I wanna pick you up and scoop you out
I want the secrets your secrets haven't found.

Paint me in trust,
I'll be your best friend,
call me the one,
this night just can't end.

Will you share your soul with me?
Unzip your skin and let me have a see.

Paint me in trust,
I'll be your best friend,
call me the one,
this night just can't end.

Oh, I'm so human;
we're just human.

Lean for me, and I'll fall back.

You'll fit so nicely, you'll keep me intact.

Paint me in trust,
I'll be your best friend,
call me the one,
this night just can't end.

I want to give you your grin
so tell me you can't bear a room that I'm not in.

Paint me in trust,
I'll be your best friend,
call me the one,
this night just can't end.

Oh, I'm so human;
we're just human.

HEARTBREAK

DAY ONE

It sits in the middle of your chest, about as heavy as a small bag of rice. You potter delicately around your space like a sad mouse; picking up and folding blankets and placing them in neat piles on the sofa. Filling up the kettle for perhaps the tenth cup of tea. Rearranging and organising and cleaning to give yourself some sort of purpose in this empty day, and also to wipe the visual triggers to limit the damage. It hurts too much to look and remember.

But the pain does come. Crying has never been so easy – you're a brimming cup of water that barely needs a knock to spill over. It is sharp, hot, raw, and it burns every hour or so. Friends are kind, and they listen. You tell the story and discover a new dramatic phrase and your throat closes up but you force out the words and heave as pals rub your back and pull you in for uncomfortably long but helpful snotty hugs. The company is so beneficial. It's not exactly what you want, of course.

You want Them.

You just want Them back.

But a back rub is a back rub, and a hug is a hug, and contact with someone you love and who loves you is healing.

DAY TWENTY

The rice bag has spilled and dispersed into the corners of your ribcage, some grains even making their way down to your fingertips and your knees. The upside is that your chest doesn't feel as weighty, but the negative side is that your entire body is in a perpetual state of discomfort, and you can't quite place your finger on why or where. The burn for Their body has mulled into a dull ache for just anyone, and the surface-level stinging has sunk into darker, colder sadness. You spend a lot of time staring in corners, the misery that used to escape through tears now running roughly through dry veins.

You start to write, which helps to pull out the buried pain and face it head on for a while. Until it starts to hurt too much again, and so you close the memory of cheeks against cheeks and hands in hair and decide only to bring it up years later, when your heart has scarred over properly. Despite it hurting so much, it's still sad that you won't feel the rawness when you decide to think of it again.

DAY FIFTY

It's all right.

The hardest bit is over. You thought it'd be impossible to get here, and now here you are. The loss doesn't hurt as much any more – but is that because you've forgotten how good it was? Are you truly healed over, or has it all just faded away?

Most likely it's a mixture of the two. You can barely remember what Their voice sounds like, Their smell, Their laugh. They still creep into your head every day, but the thought doesn't make your heart stop and your hands clench. Maybe you'll find someone new. Maybe They already have. That still hurts, of course – the idea that someone else can make them happier than you could.

But the best part is, you're starting to realise that it was never going to work. The rose-tinted view of the relationship fades away as the magic has, and suddenly you start seeing it for what it was – flawed but, most of all, not special. All the advice and concerns people gave that you waved away as irrelevant, because they 'don't understand, this is different', now start to make sense, and you realise that you and your relationship went through all the stereotypes and you didn't even notice.

What a strange being you are.
God knows where I would be
if you hadn't found me
sitting all alone in the dark.

A dumb screenshot of youth;
watch how a cold broken teen
will desperately lean on a superglued human of proof.

What the hell would I be
without you?
Brave face talk so lightly,
hide the truth.

'Cause I'm sick of losing soulmates,
so where do we begin?
I can finally see
you're as fucked up as me;
so how do we win?

Yeah, I'm sick of losing soulmates;
won't be alone again.
I can finally see
you're as fucked up as me,
so how do we win?

We will grow old as friends.
I've promised that before
so what's one more?
In our grey-haired circle, waiting for the end.

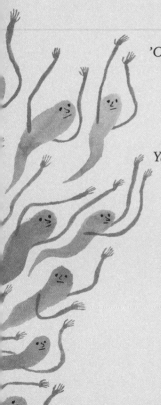

Time and hearts will wear us thin,
so which path will you take?
'Cause we both know a break
does exactly what it says on the tin.

What the hell would I be
without you?
Brave face talk so lightly,
hide the truth.

'Cause I'm sick of losing soulmates,
so where do we begin?
I can finally see
you're as fucked up as me;
so how do we win?

Yeah, I'm sick of losing soulmates;
won't be alone again.
I can finally see
you're as fucked up as me;
so how do we win?

I won't take no for an answer.

TIPS

THEY ARE NOT YOUR IDENTITY

When I was going through my first proper breakup of a relationship of two years, I remember my mum coming into my bedroom to find me weeping over a pair of his boxers he'd lent me as pyjama bottoms.

'I just don't know who I am without him,' I sobbed.

And, for a while, I didn't. It felt as though I had knitted myself into someone gradually over time and then been ripped in half so suddenly. It felt too strange to know that he was talking about things to his other friends in his now separate world that I would never hear or help him with. And I was carrying so much in my head that I'd usually pour out to him; but of course my go-to guy for heartbreak was now the cause of it, so instead I'd give out little bits of my pain to different friends and family instead. But I was so used to having a partner in crime, just two main people in my team of life. His name belonged with an 'and Dodie', and I'd whisper those three words and try to comprehend that it was now just me.

I had known him so well. I could have played his part out in a conversation, and I could hear his laugh and his voice when I came across something I knew he'd have enjoyed. My phone buzzed familiarly and I expected to see his name flash up on the top of the screen, but it was never him any more. I wondered when the next time I'd hear someone say 'I love you' again would be, and it was impossible to believe that it wouldn't come from him.

But here I am, years later, and the idea of him, or anyone, being a part of my identity now is laughable. There are good people who will stay in your life, but even then they won't be a part of you; you will wear their loyalty and kindness like armour, and they will add strength to your existence and build you up. You can lean on these people now and again, but they cannot hold you up all the time, and you certainly can't expect just one person to on their own either.

You are you, and you are wonderful. It will be hard to be with just yourself again, but now you can pour your love, care and attention solely into the number one priority in your life: you.

THIS WON'T HURT FOREVER

'Think of it like a tunnel.'

The heating in Sammy's empty family house in Bristol had been cut off before the day of the move, so we lay by his fireplace, warming our feet up in front of the flames. My tears dripped down my cheeks and into my ears.

'The other side is beautiful, bright and pain free. All your friends – including me' – he grinned – 'are standing at the end, waving, smiling and shouting directions and encouragement at you from the sunshine. But you have to walk through this cold, damp, dark tunnel to get there.

'There will be days where you will run through, bounding your way to us. And then there will be days where you'll just want to run back, because it's closer than the exit. It will be horrible, and scary, and different; but bit by bit you'll make your way through, and then you'll come out the other side and we'll all still be with you, and you won't even remember what it was like before.'

I turned my face to look at him, and a sentence appeared in my brain that hurt so much my eyes welled up dramatically.

'But what if I can't walk forward, and I stay in the tunnel forever?' I mumbled pathetically, my throat closing up and tears spilling down my neck.

* * *

It's hard to relate to past me; someone who couldn't comprehend the idea that I wouldn't always feel as sad about the person I was leaving behind. I knew that I had to move on to new chapters in my life, and I wanted to, but I didn't know if I could. I was terrified that to get over a relationship was just to forget what it was like, and I didn't want that!

I like to make deep and intense connections. I spend years getting to know people I enjoy intimately, and I dig underneath the surface and we scoop out our secrets and inner thoughts and share them with each other; so to say goodbye to someone I had shared my soul with for so long felt so unnatural and terrible for me.

But Sammy had been right. The tunnel was terrible for the first month, and then it got brighter, and then I pretty much forgot I was walking through one until it was half a year later and I realised I had already been out the other side for a while.

I have felt that pain three different times in my life, and despite each new broken heart insisting it would be even more impossible to mend than the last one, they have all healed over time.

THIS WAS THE RIGHT DECISION

There is always some relief in a breakup. Everything that ends, ends for a reason, and if you can't find one yet, you'll come across it later. The sooner you understand that, the sooner you can start making your journey through the tunnel of breaking up that leads to being better. People are going to tell you that 'you have so much time' to find someone else, and that 'there are plenty of fish in the sea'. And, for a while, you're going to say you don't want someone else, you want that particular fish, because no one else will have all the wonderful qualities that they had that made you fall in love with them.

But – to quote my first boyfriend, actually – life is a bus ride, with only so many seats. It took me a long time to comprehend that sometimes people had to leave my life, to make room for the better ones, but once I understood that it became easier to let go, and I was surprised at just how quickly new, interesting people somehow found their way onto my bus.

Your friends are usually right, in the end; if a relationship is damaging you, they will be able to see it much more clearly than you will. And you might argue that they're wrong, you might even manage to convince yourself, but there will always be a part of you that knows; and in the end you should hold on to it as a way to guide you out of this. If it's a perfect, happy goodbye, then good; you've got yourself some closure. And if it's terrible, then good; let that be a reminder of why this is happening.

Close the book; it is finished, and it served its purpose. You loved, you broke, and you will learn for when you next love again.

I KNEW YOU ONCE

I knew you once
and it was nice.
I knew your brain and your heart,
all your insides.

Oh, I could tell
just with a look
what you were thinking,
that's all it took.

You shared your secrets
and I shared mine.
Silence was comfy
without having to try.

We swapped our smiles,
gifted advice,
yes, I knew you once
and it was nice.

PROCESSING

All right, look. It's 9.16 p.m. and you've had one glass of white wine with your dinner. You're going through old hard drives for some reason – you're editing a video and you need some footage from your old laptop; you're trying to prove a point to a friend about a discussion from months ago – or it's 9.16 p.m. and you've had wine and you're just bloody nostalgic. You're searching through folders, letting out little chuckles at past conversations and bad haircuts, sipping from your glass, and suddenly you see it and your heart drops. You click away immediately – a well-trained knee-jerk reaction. You've blocked them on all their social media, but of course their face still crops up now and again and you're well used to scrolling past quickly, pushing the pain away. But this is different – a snapshot of a happy, love-filled time. This picture of them will be the familiar version, the face of someone you loved, someone who loved you.

Do you look?

Are you allowed?

Has it been long enough?

You reckon you can handle it. You're strong enough now, surely. You brace yourself, and open the file.

You're surprised. It doesn't hurt as much as you thought it would; in fact, it makes you smile. You picture the memory, and the events around that night. There was a little argument in the car on the way there about who came up with that funny joke you both told to friends, you had held hands under the table and took it in turns to squeeze, you had tripped over the kerb on your way walking back and they had laughed. You stare into your younger eyes, trying to relate to the person whose heart was attached to the soul standing next to them, but you honestly find it difficult. These two people were happy together, here; but now neither of these versions of them exists, and this photo belongs to the past, before time had changed the world in the wonderful way it did.

DUMPED IN DISNEYLAND

I'm chewing on a straw to distract myself from the ache in the soles of my feet and my chest. The sharpness of the plastic against my tongue also helps to ground my existence; as usual, my brain decides for me that a way to deal with the pain is to shut off reality and numb every other sense.

I am so sad. I haven't been this sad for such a long time, and so the universe thought it would be funny to place me in the brightest, most saturated happy place in the world and place cold hands around my throat, my heart, my brain, and squeeze, just a little. I let my eyes unfocus, and the voices and chuckles around me fade away and I let it all just swallow me up. I don't care that I look sour-faced, that I've paid $200 to stand in a hot queue and feel shit, that maybe if I tried really, REALLY hard I could push it all away and choose to at least try and enjoy myself. But I have no energy left to tread water right now.

I can't even cry. It's so deep rooted I can't find a way to bring it to the surface, and so it just sits inside, weighing my body down and rotting my soul.

I fade in out of time. In one of my zoning-out moments I hear a sharp voice: 'Dodie?'

I look up, suddenly aware that I was letting my cheeks droop, and I probably look stupid.

'Can I take a picture with you?' A girl in pigtails is smiling at me. I pull my cheeks up with the little energy I have and try to reflect the tone of her voice. 'Sure!'

We stand together and I look at someone in their phone screen with my face who is showing their teeth but their eyes are dead. She takes the picture. I wonder whether I should tell her.

'Thank you!' She hugs her phone and twirls away.

'I feel terrible,' I murmur. She spins around again and laughs awkwardly, still walking away. That was a mistake.

She brushes past a couple in the queue. There's a women wearing white, lacy ears and she has a badge that says 'happily ever after!' in a font that reminds me of primary school. She's holding her partner's hand loosely, their fingers interlocking. Her mouth is upturned, her eyes glossy. She darts her head around, clearly drinking in and relishing the situation around her. My eyes immediately fill with tears – but not because I'm jealous.

One day, I will be standing in Disneyland with white ears and a happy badge. I'll be holding someone's arm, smiling up at the world around me. The grey memories of now will be tied up in a little box, and they will sit somewhere in the back of my mind, available enough to visit if I need to but far away enough for them not to hurt me. I will be an entirely different woman – someone who is not in pain, and someone who cannot relate to the numb, cold, sad girl that I am now.

She feels so far away that she must be impossible. The pain is so real right now that it feels like I will be this girl forever. But I know that that can't be true.

I chew on my straw and blink back tears, breathing in a mixture of hope, depression and hurt.

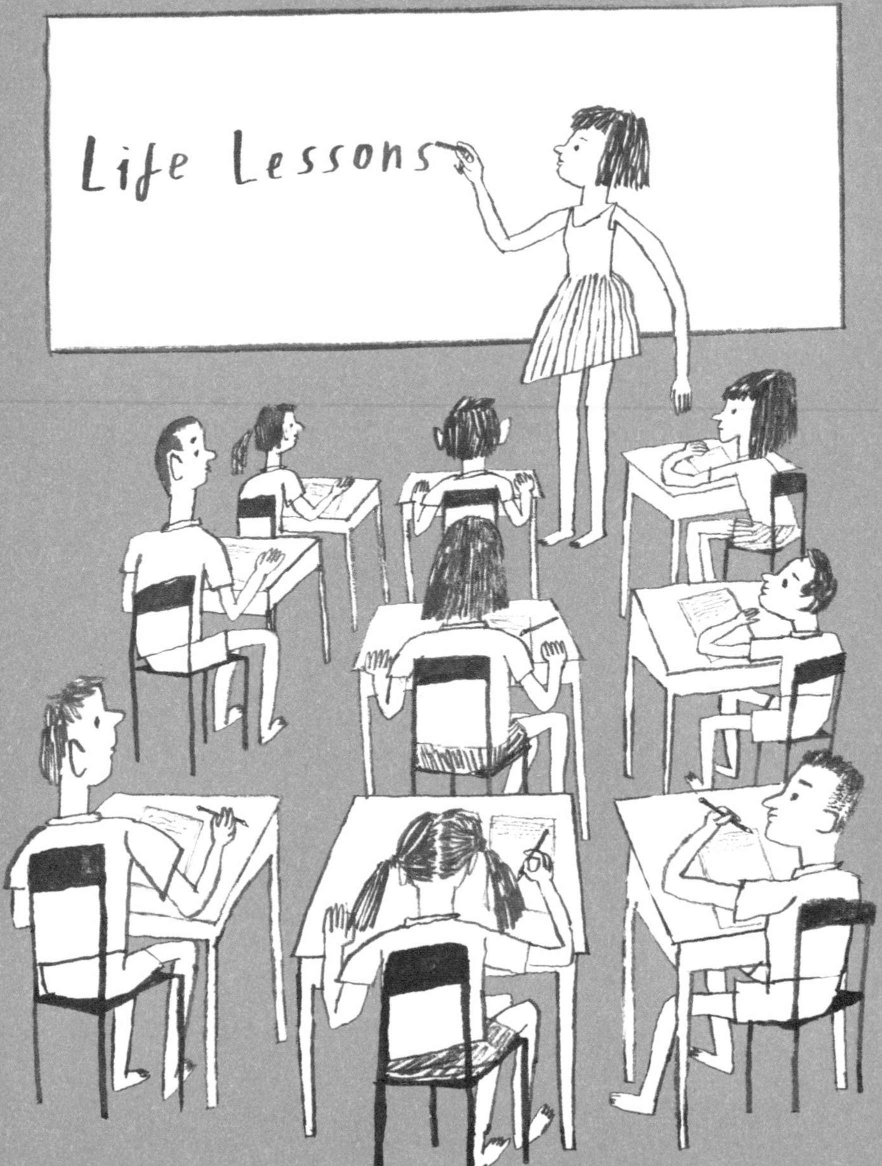
Life Lessons

When I'm eighty years old, and alone in my chair,
will I look back at safety, and be glad I didn't care?

NO! I can hear her screaming, 'Love, break and learn!
What else are you young for?! FUCK IT! Hurt whilst you can!'

LOVE ♡

BREAK 💔

LEARN 💔

BISEXUALITY
– COMING OUT TO MYSELF

I was twelve, and she was adorable. She had thick orange and gold locks that tumbled down her back, little straight white teeth that peeked out of her pink smile, and cocoa powder freckles on cotton skin. I'd beg her to draw on my arm with a biro pen and I'd get tingles running up the back of my neck as I felt her cold skinny fingers on my wrist and drank in her smell of apples and a dusting of talcum powder. I'd gravitate to wherever she was, following her around and laughing extra loud just so she'd look at me and smile back.

But she was just older, and cooler. I wasn't confused, or worried, or guilty – I would grow up and have boyfriends and marry a man. I fancied Tom Downey in Mr Potter's class. The joy and ache I got from looking at this girl felt so normal I was certain it was just something everyone experienced. The word 'gay' was a naughty, shocking word, and I'd never have anything to do with it.

* * *

'He's bisexual,' Alice exclaimed, wide-eyed and cross-legged on my bedroom floor. It sounded dirty, and I was sceptical and worried for her. Boys kissing boys = gay, and the popular people found it bad. What was she doing, fancying someone like that? At least he didn't go to our school.

I didn't really get it. He was so nice, and he seemed so normal. Now he was weird.

We scuffed our school shoes on the ground as we walked around the basketball court, guilt sinking into my stomach. Charlotte, another girl at my school, had just told me that she fancied girls, and in a state of awkwardness I told her I felt the same. A rush of panic came over me as I realised I was walking next to a LESBIAN. Did she fancy me? Was she going to tell everyone that I was one too?!

'They're just so . . . soft. And they smell nice. They're so pretty,' I said.

I couldn't tell if I was lying or not. Everything I was saying was definitely true; but she was so certain, while I felt sick at the idea of everyone knowing. My friends would think I fancied them, but I didn't! I didn't even know if I fancied girls properly. I was sure that everyone got the same type of crushes on girls that I did, and that Charlotte was actually different, so I must have been lying. So I told her about all the girls I'd fancied and we gushed over the relatability of secretly fancying people, somehow telling the truth while the words 'I'M NOT GAY' screamed at me from the bottom of my brain.

* * *

I didn't want to commit to the label in my late teens. The fear of the word 'gay' had thankfully dissolved as I transcended from the judgemental crowds of Essex to friendlier, love-based communities from the internet. After experiencing female kisses at drunken parties, I knew that I definitely enjoyed being intimate with women, but even so, I was convinced that it didn't mean I deserved a different label, as everyone must feel the same way I did. How could anyone not want to? We were all just hiding it, and soon enough me and my other schoolfriends would be laughing about the days we didn't admit that we fancied girls as well as boys.

Turns out I was the only one in my friendship circle who ended up admitting it because none of them actually felt the same as I did. Apparently, a lot of the female population didn't either, and those who did might label themselves as bisexual.

So I took the label, and I loved it. I love that I have the capacity to fall in love with anyone, regardless of gender, and I love that, actually, I am different to a lot of people I know. I love that, through the label, I found people whom I can relate to, and I love that I am part of a community that needs more attention. It took me a while to find out who I was, and there was nothing wrong with that for me, but perhaps my journey would have been a little smoother if I had grown up in a world where the word 'bisexual' wasn't so terrifying.

Nevertheless, I love it. I am lucky that I can love my sexuality, and love myself, and I will strive for a world in which everyone can feel the same.

SHE

Am I allowed to look at her like that?
Could it be wrong when she's just so nice to look at?

And she smells like lemongrass and sleep,
she tastes like apple juice and peach.
You would find her in a Polaroid picture
and she means everything to me.

I'd never tell,
no, I'd never say a word,
and oh, it aches,
but it feels oddly good to hurt.

She smells like lemongrass and sleep,
she tastes like apple juice and peach.
You would find her in a Polaroid picture
and she means everything to me.

And I'll be okay
admiring from afar
'cause even when she's next to me
we could not be more far apart.
'Cause she tastes like birthday cake and storytime and fall,
but to her
I taste of nothing at all.

And she smells like lemongrass and sleep,
she tastes like apple juice and peach.
You would find her in a Polaroid picture
and she means everything to me.

she

FAME

I'm not too sure if I deserve the title of famous. Let me google the definition:

famous
1.
known about by many people.

Well. Yes. I guess so.

2.
informal
excellent.
'Galway stormed to a famous victory'

HA. Not too sure about that one, Google. Especially because there are many famous people who are far from excellent.

* * *

By my younger standards, I'm famous. I don't really know how child me created such a clear definition, but I remember thinking of it as very black or white. Fame was akin to having magical powers – you either had magic, or you didn't, and I wanted it more than anything. This absolutely stemmed from my insecurities that came from bullying: the desire to be liked, and to be special, and I begged my parents to take me to drama clubs and dance classes so I could one day be loved as much as I loved the 'famous' people I knew. I'd see West End shows for my birthdays, and I'd lean forward in my seat, gazing up at the performers and wondering when they'd notice that someone potentially magical was waiting to be invited up to dance. We'd wait by the stage door and I'd hold out my ticket and a pen to the 'famous people', staring at their skin and wondering if they were truly real. They'd float away, probably to their mansions, and I'd fall asleep in the car home, dreaming of the other world they lived in and clutching my bag stuffed with confetti from the show as if it was valuable fairy dust.

* * *

When I was nine years old, I got a letter from my drama club asking me if I wanted to participate in the Lord Mayor's Show parade as a dancer. This wasn't like any old ballet show – I would be performing to thousands and thousands of strangers. I was taught a routine, given balloons to hold, and told to smile and wave as we marched by. I obviously didn't need much encouragement. I extended my limbs in my steps and stretched my smile as wide as it could go. My legs burned and my cheeks ached, but I was on the other side. 'I'm famous!' I squealed to the older dancers around me, who laughed as I waved and blew kisses ecstatically to the London public. I felt special, and adored, and though the next day I'd wander around the playground alone, singing to myself as my classmates played in the groups around me, for one day I felt wanted.

* * *

When I was fourteen, I wrote a song called 'green grass'.

Look at them smiling,
they're living the life.
That grass is so green
on the other side.

If I had that chance I could so easily be there,
but whilst they're living my dream, I don't think they care.
Do they even know how lucky they are?
To be where that green grass grows – to be a star.

My curiosity and desire for fame had led me to obsessive watching of behind-the-scenes videos of Disney Channel stars on YouTube. I could quote Selena Gomez and Demi Lovato's private jokes down to their intonation and pauses, and I would waltz around my room mimicking an American accent and telling my toys that I 'loved seeing Miley at the DC meeting yesterday'. (Yes, I was a weird kid. Surely we've established that by now.) The friendship that they broadcasted online was just like mine and Alice's, and I knew that we'd all be best friends, if only we could somehow meet. I remember being so jealous, and angry. Mum would tell me that the kids on Disney Channel were pushed into acting classes from a young age and were forced to audition before they could write, and I was so irritated that I'd missed out on the life I wanted because my parents didn't do that for me. So I wrote bitter songs about my dumb normal life at school and continued to dream about me and my cool famous friends, rocking up to shoots and waving to our fans outside hotel rooms.

From the Disney Channel videos, I started finding and watching other people who made 'vlogs' and who had an audience. There was Shane Dawson and all of his friends, DaveDays, WhatTheBuck, Rhett and Link and then Charlieissocoollike, Lukeisnotsexy, Musicalbethan and the whole British crew – I'd watch them all religiously, absolutely infatuated with each of their worlds and desperate to break through the barrier and make contact with the side of the famous. I'd do anything to get their attention – even just thinking that their eyes had seen my username and that therefore I was somehow included in their memories was enough. They'd do livestreams and I'd change my font to a bright colour, type in all caps and absolutely spam the chat box, trying to shout above the other hundreds and hundreds of fans who were trying to get noticed. But it felt like I was drowned out, that we were all just screaming at someone who was untouchable. It really was as if they were living in a different world, and my quest to gain their attention was a subconscious need to prove that they were real. I guess I thought of them the same way as I did with characters in a cartoon, or series, and though they'd say that they 'didn't share everything online' I was convinced, having absorbed their content so much, I knew them better than anyone.

* * *

In 2011 a particular favourite YouTuber of mine and the band he was in were doing a signing in London. I flipped out.

I wrote a letter with a purple pen about how me and my little sister would dance around the house to his songs, wrapped a £20 note inside to buy the album, and travelled into London with a schoolfriend to spend the day queuing outside with hundreds of other fans. One girl told me she knew him, and that she'd hung out with him and his mum a few months ago. I stuck to her like glue.

After hours of boasting to others about my knowledge of YouTubers and singing along to people struggling to play ukulele in the cold, it was our turn to head inside. As I handed a security guard my ticket, my heart rose to my throat, and I was suddenly worried I was going to vomit. We shuffled in and *I saw three-dimensional, real faces of people I knew so well from a screen. They looked into my eyes and smiled and my mouth went dry and my legs went stiff and my brain started short circuiting and I stuttered a hello and shakily handed over my letter and tried to say something funny but it didn't come out right and I gave them my CD to sign and one of them offered me a grape and I almost thought about taking one and not eating it so I could keep it forever and then the security hurried us along and they were already starting to say hello to the next group that came in so I said goodbye and none of them turned their heads and then the door closed behind us and it was over.* I immediately burst into tears.

Meeting someone who felt so special to me was honestly painful, and the feeling of being drowned out by other fans was amplified immensely in real life. I went over everything I said and did, regretting my awkward words and shaky hands, and I sank further away from the green grass world of the people I idolised. I was just another silly, cringey fangirl, and it hurt.

So I wrote about it.

I'm not quite sure
what I should do,
I'm ever so
in love with you.
Wine gums and juggling
and haircuts and tea,
and oh, my heart leaps each time you look at me.

But I have to stop
and clear my head.
Your eyes don't meet mine,
they meet a camera instead,
and even though I know you
like you're mine,
I'm a stranger to you,
a fan who screams all the time.
But I say

Charlieissocoollike, one day you'll be my friend,
and we'll sing your duet and I will bet that my happiness will not
end, but a million other people share this beautiful dream,
so I'll never be Miss Coollike after all, so it seems.

Oh, the awkward endings and the ukulele,
the mustache poems and the . . . (what rhymes with ukulele?)
I know that we'd get along like a house on fire
and it seems you agree,
each time you smile.

But I have to stop
and clear my head.
Your eyes don't meet mine,
they meet a camera instead,
and even though I know you
like you're mine,

I'm a stranger to you,
a fan who squeals all the time.
But I say

Charlieissocoollike, one day you'll be my friend,
and we'll sing your duet and I will bet that my happiness will not
end, but a million other people share this beautiful dream,
so I'll never be Miss Coollike after all, so it seems.

I've only met you once, and I acted like a fool,
I was shaking like a leaf and you said 'ahh, cool!'
You looked at me and grinned in your very cool like way,
I was imagining dopamine released inside your awesome brain,
but as I left, I stared outside and hopefuls too who queued all day,
my face would soon be forgotten, as would the others who feel the
same way.

And yet I still believe that you'll remember me,
so while I watch you every day, I guess I'll still say,

Charlieissocoollike, one day you'll be my friend,
and we'll sing your duet and I will bet that my happiness will not
end, but a million other people share this beautiful dream,
so I'll never be Miss Coollike after all, so it seems.

I can't even LOOK at this without gaining twenty chins from cringing so much. Beautiful dream?! Vom.

But it matches up to my memory; my view of fame was still black and white, as I said before, and life had placed me in the less fortunate side. I'd forever be pining for attention from those 'more important' than me, and it hurt so much to feel as though I was just part of a statistic. But I used my pain to make something. I didn't write it with any sort of goal; I suppose if there was one, it was for the other people in the queue. Of course I had a small hope that he'd find it, but that felt so impossible with all the years of reaching and failing. I clearly belonged in the unpopular side of the world – school had also made that clear – and so I settled there.

The YouTuber I met found my song about him, and commented something kind about how he was 'definitely going to remember me now!' My dad shouted at me for filling the house with screams – but I'd done it. I'd somehow pushed through to the other world – it did exist! And even though it was something so small, I felt like I was a part of it.

I kept writing and making videos. There were a few people who had found my song about being a fan, and I'd notice them commenting on each of my posts to say that they'd shared it with their best friend, or their mum, and we'd all write back to each other, expressing excited mutual thanks. The amount of people watching the things I made grew, but I tried my best to reply to every kind comment anyone had left. The popular boys in my school would tease me – 'Look, it's Doddleoddle! Hey, are you famous, Dodie?' – and they'd play my videos on the projector while I squealed at them to turn it off, secretly excited at the idea that, to them, a thousand views meant fame. I don't know if it did; I still felt just as far away from the green grass lifestyles of truly famous people as I ever had been. I wasn't being stopped on the street, and I certainly wasn't rich, but I did have a little community of people who would cover my songs, write me letters, and even draw pictures of me.

I am still confused about the definition of fame, but I know that it is certainly nowhere near as black and white as I used to think. The world seems to think fame comes along with perfection, money and happiness, but that isn't true at all (not that it isn't fun, of course; but the part I enjoy is the connection, and recognition and appreciation for what I make, not just the label or the idea that people would recognise my face). The point is, according to my younger self, I live on the other side of the grass now. It should be bright green, and all of my problems should be gone, but as I was growing, the thick line between what I thought was fame and not fame kept rising as my life didn't match the expectations I'd had for it all. I sat in this weird middle ground, and I started to realise that the step after achieving fame is maintaining relevancy. If you make fame your goal, you will never truly be happy because you will constantly be reaching for something that isn't sustainable.

I strove for fame because I was desperate for it to make me happy, but in doing so I accidentally found what really made me feel fulfilled: learning, growing, creating and sharing. Still, I am proud I got to experience everything my younger self had ached for. I've played giant shows to people who sing my lyrics loudly with me, I get stopped in the street multiple times if I'm walking around a central area, and I've met thousands and thousands of people who have handed me heartfelt letters after waiting in queues, just as I did in 2011. Whenever people's hands shake, or they tell me how strange it is to see me in real life, I want to tell them, 'I know! I know it so well. But believe me, I am not magical! I still get anxious, I still make mistakes, and I too still wait in queues for a chance to say hi to someone who I respect.' There's never enough time, and I can never find the perfect words in the moment to thank them for listening to me, but I try my best, because I am so grateful.

Life didn't gift me with fame when I was younger (thank goodness), despite my bitterness about feeling as though I was owed it for some reason. It is important to remember that my goal should always be to improve, whether that is artistically or as a person. I didn't understand for a long time that that happens first, and then fame might come along with it, rather than fame automatically making people great. People might stop listening and that's okay, because happiness should not come from the amount of people who know you, but it can come from pride in your work. And, as it turns out, if you enjoy what you make, there will most likely be other people who do too.

COOKING

'HELLO! HELP!' you say.

'What the heck do people eat when they live somewhere far away from parental guardianship and they have to feed themselves?' you say.

'Don't get me wrong, I love frozen fish fingers and ketchup, but I haven't actually pooped in three days and I don't think I'm putting enough good stuff into my body but I don't know how to make it taste good!' you say.

HAVE NO FEAR.

Despite me being an absolute mess in all other domestic categories, I'm not too shabby at cooking. I think part of it is because I possibly burned off most of my taste buds eating fizzy sweets when I was younger, and so I pretty much chuck every sort of seasoning I can in because that's the only way I can taste something.

Also, cooking is my down time. It's a mindful task; you have no option but to live in the moment, otherwise you'll accidentally chop a finger off. But it's such a wonderful way to unwind – to take in the smells of fruits, herbs, garlic, and if you're making a meal for other people too, you get the reward of hearing happy munches and the satisfaction of gratitude after your care.

A HANDY SHOPPING LIST:

* oil to cook stuff in. Olive oil or coconut oil is perfect!

* bread, eggs, milk, butter. Or your flatmate will not be best pleased

* vegetables! Onions, peppers, courgettes (zucchini), tomatoes, aubergines (eggplant) for frying, then lettuce, spring onions, cucumbers and carrots for snacking and salads. Avocado if you're feeling millennial

* pasta, potatoes, rice. Oh, beautiful carbohydrates

* generic tomato pasta sauce, pesto – stuff to chuck on said beautiful carbohydrates

* salt and pepper, for when everything goes wrong and you can trick everyone into thinking it's delicious

* meat! Or fake meat!

BREAKFASTS

HEALTHY BREAKFAST WRAP

You will need!

* wholewheat tortilla wrap (apparently wholewheat is healthier. I'm not too sure why – but honestly I prefer the flavour. It's breadier.)

* eggs

* chopped veggies! Onions, peppers, courgettes, etc – mushrooms if you want, but goodness WHY?

* vegetarian mince (or normal mince, of course, but I hate cooking with meat)(ground beef/vegetarian substitute)

* tomato pasta sauce

* cheese

* avocado and lettuce

* ketchup and hot sauce if you would like!

1. Scramble those eggs! Crack them in a bowl, whisk them up and then pour them into a pan that's been melting some butter. If you leave these on a low heat, they can cook slowly, which makes them even more delicious while you do everything else. Make sure you stir them every now and again though! And don't forget to add some salt and pepper. Bland eggs is a great band name but not good for breakfast.

2. Fry the veggies and the mince until they're almost soft, and then add in a spoonful of tomato pasta sauce.

3. Microwave your tortilla wraps so they're nice and warm! Grate your cheese, slice up your avo, and then bring everything out in this-looks-fancy-but-mostly-assemble-it-yourself style. Laugh at how your friends fail to estimate how much can fit in one burrito and enjoy your tasty breakfast!

POACHED EGGS AND SALAD

This is so simple it doesn't really need a 'you will need' list. Here's how to poach an egg!

Bring some water to the boil, and then turn it off, so the water is still. Add in a tiny capful of white wine vinegar (no worries if you don't have that – it apparently just helps to keep the egg in place) and carefully crack an egg into the middle. Then, leave it sitting in the hot water for about seven minutes. While that's doing its thing, toast some wholewheat bread and prepare your salad: chop up some lettuce, cucumbers, tomatoes, avocado and green onions, and mix it all about in a big bowl with some lemon juice, olive oil, salt and pepper. Arrange this how you would like on your plate, and then grab a slotted spoon and carefully fish out your egg. It SHOULD be the perfect amount of soft, so slop it on your toast and salad, set up your phone for a slow mo/boomerang and cut into your egg for that mouth-watering yolk goop.

LUNCHES

HOMEMADE RAMEN

You will need!

* noodles of some kind! Rice noodles, ramen noodles, tagliatelle – whichever you fancy

* yellow, red, or orange peppers (is it just me or do green peppers taste slightly more bitter?)

* red chillies, garlic, ginger, coriander, baby spinach, spring onions

* spinach

* vegetable stock cube

* lime!

1. Boil your noodles in just enough water to cover them. Leave them to cook for about eight minutes while you chop up everything else, and then crumble in a vegetable stock cube to make it salty.

2. Add in the peppers and chillies, cook for a further few minutes, and then scrape in the chopped garlic, ginger and coriander. Cook for another few minutes until everything is soft, and then turn off the heat and add in a few handfuls of spinach.

3. Roll your juicy lime (I beg your pardon), cut it in half, and then squeeze it through your hands into the mixture. Stir well and serve your spicy, salty, tangy sweet noodles! Yum!

MAC AND CHEESE

Again, this one doesn't really need a list of ingredients. Just make sure you have cheese.

Boil some water, crack in some sea salt and pour in your macaroni. While that cooks, melt a chunk of butter in a pan. Add a few tablespoons of flour till it turns into a weird paste (a ROUX if you want to feel French), and then pour in milk a bit at a time, to make a creamy sauce. Add some salt and pepper, and then add a LOT of grated cheese and just a wee bit of mustard. Boom! Add in your drained pasta, and serve with garlic bread and salad to make you feel less guilty.

DINNERS

Delicious evening meals with friends

You will need!

* a high street nearby with a choice of many restaurants.

Alternatively,

* a kind pal to cook for you. For example, a Daniel J. Layton.

(Dan will take it from here!)

VEGGIE BOLOGNESE FOR FOUR

The ultimate comfort food. You've had a bad day, you're feeling a little off kilter and you're looking for familiar, welcoming flavours to transport you to tranquil zen . . . ness – you can't do better than this.

You will need!

* olive oil

* a red onion

* a clove of garlic. Make it a hefty one because garlic is delicious.

* an unsettlingly phallic carrot

* a handful of mushrooms (Dodie, don't cut that bit – they're delicious and you're wrong)

* a glass of red, red wine (optional but worth it)

* 350g portion of veggie mince

* 400g can chopped tomatoes

* balsamic vinegar (we're getting fancy, mate)

* dried oregano

1. Finely chop your onion. This might make you cry, so feel free to let out actual emotions and then pretend you're actually fine. Then compose yourself while dicing the carrot and slicing the mushrooms.

2. Drizzle some oil in a large frying pan over a medium heat, then fry the onion and carrot, until the onions have softened and turned a delightful pink. Crush in the garlic and add the mushrooms, cooking for a bit before pouring in your wine and letting it simmer for just under five minutes until it's cooked down a bit. You'll have a load of wine left in the bottle. Down it. (Don't.) (Unless you want to.) (No, actually, don't.)

3. Add the veggie mince and give it a good stir, then pour in the chopped tomatoes. Half fill the can with some water, then swill it (gross) so you get all the tomato-y goodness before that goes in the pan too. Stir it to make a sauce, bring it to the boil, and enjoy the bubbles before lowering the heat and letting it simmer until it thickens slightly (about ten minutes).

4. Splosh in about a teaspoon of balsamic vinegar and sprinkle over a smattering of oregano to round out the sauce and season to taste.

5. Serve with pasta of your choice (obv spaghetti is proper, but I'm keen on its thicker cousin tagliatelle, which makes, delightfully, Tag Bol . . .), a bowlful of grated cheddar and a plate piled high with garlic bread, because . . . mate. Mate, though.

VEGGIE CHILLI FOR FOUR

You can make this as hot as you like by leaving the chilli seeds in, or by adding more if you're a maverick. I like a bit of a kick, but Dodes and pals can't handle more than a slight, warm tingling so I only use one. Unless I fancy a laugh.

You will need!

* olive oil

* a nice chunky sweet potato

* a red onion

* a red chilli, deseeded

* a clove of garlic (see above)

* a couple o' peppers (one red, one yellow, for aesthetic purposes)

* two 400g cans chopped tomatoes

* two 400g cans kidney beans, drained

* one teaspoon each of cumin, cinnamon, cayenne pepper

* three cubes dark chocolate (no, seriously)

1. Peel the sweet potato and chop it into bite-size cubes. Toss with olive oil and a sprinkling of salt and pepper, then spread evenly on a baking tray. Roast in an oven at 200°C (if you want that in Fahrenheit, you should have thought about that before you bought this book) for forty minutes, turning halfway. Set aside to add right at the end.

2. Chop your onion, garlic, chilli and peppers, then fry over a medium heat until soft. Add your spices and cook for a minute. You aren't even slightly ready for how good this will smell.

3. Add the kidney beans followed by the chopped tomatoes and give it a good stir. Add a little water if you think it needs it, then bring to the boil, reduce the heat and simmer for about twenty minutes.

4. Chuck in the cubes of dark chocolate. Trust me, chocolate and chilli is a match made in heaven – it adds a beautiful depth and sweet roundness to the tangy sauce.

5. Add the roasted cubes of sweet potato and BOOM. Nailed it.

6. Serve with rice and some form of bread. I go with garlic naan. Mild culture clash, sure, but I reckon both continents would be absolutely on board.

DEAR HEDY

Mum told me she was pregnant as a way to cheer me up when I was eight years old and sick in bed with one of my stomach migraines. It was the old red bowl, half-sipped glasses of old water and loo roll by the bed deal; I was sleeping, throwing up, crying, repeating – weak, miserable and dramatic. I half sat up on top of mountains of pillows while Mum stroked my limp dry arms and softly chatted to me through the nausea.

'I have something that might cheer you up,' she said with a smile, a sparkle in her eye. As a particularly excitable child, this was one of the best things to hear, and I immediately perked up. Sweeties? A booked trip to a theme park? What was this secret?!

'You have to promise not to tell anyone, for a while. No one at school. Not even Lauren, or Natasha.'

I nodded as enthusiastically as I could for someone whose insides were rolling around. She smirked and looked away, dragging out the process as long as possible, until I was ready to burst. Either with vomit or curiosity, I couldn't really tell. She looked back at me, opened her mouth, held it there for a bit, and then whispered, 'I'm pregnant!'

For a split second I was confused. And then the widest grin grew across my face. 'Really?'

Mum nodded.

In all honesty, I was a little too young and definitely too sick to process this information properly. I knew I was excited, but I didn't really know what for, or what was going to happen.

I got better, went back to school and ended up accidentally telling Lauren. And Natasha. And Jessica, Ella, Sophie, Ms Harris and pretty much everyone in year four. Top tip: don't tell a kid with an obsession about gaining attention a potential attention-attracting secret. I'd drag my friends and teachers to meet my mum in the playground after school, dancing around her and babbling, 'Here she is! Look! There's a baby in that tummy!' ecstatic that there was something so new and interesting happening in my life. Mum tutted at me for spreading her secret; she was only twelve weeks pregnant and that information wasn't something to share until a little later, especially because she'd had a miscarriage a year or so before. But she was excited too, and chatted to Ms Harris a little after her confused (slightly forced by me) congratulations.

* * *

As you probably know, little Dodie's world was driven by her ginormous imagination. I started planning the worlds we would explore, the tricks we'd play on Iain, dreamed of us swapping clothes, painting each other's nails, sharing wishes and secrets. The nine-year age gap didn't faze me in the slightest, as I'd already chosen never to grow up and so that would obviously never be an issue. I started watching documentaries on pregnancy and childbirth, reading books on becoming a mum and practising nappy changing on all my dolls. I'd sing to you through Mum's large belly and think of you smiling inside, knowing that you'd recognise my voice when you arrived.

There was also, however, a slight worry. I knew that I loved my family in a very different sort of way to my friends. The love I had for Mum and Dad, Iain, Granny and Granddad, Grandma – it was rooted deeper in my soul and I'd known it forever. You were to be a stranger, and I didn't know if I was capable of experiencing that same sort of love for someone I hadn't met yet. I was so excited for you to come, but what if I didn't love you the same way? What if I didn't love you enough?

* * *

I met you in Mum and Dad's room in a tiny cradle by the bed. You had white cotton mittens, pink gums and a tiny button nose. You wrapped your little hand around my finger. I definitely loved you enough.

* * *

I seemed to have skipped over the years of you being a baby in my plans and fantasies, but nevertheless enjoyed bottle feeding you and teaching you words. I tried playing teatime with you when you were just over two, but you just slid off your chair and threw the plastic cups across the room.

'She's still a bit too young for this, I think,' Mum tried to comfort me when I folded my arms and pouted. 'Just wait a few more years.'

Well, somehow my 'never growing up' thing didn't really work out, and there wasn't too much of an overlap of us both wanting to play together. By the time you were ready and longing to have a dressing-up tea party with me, I was fourteen and wanted mostly to talk about boys in my room with Alice. You'd wander in and steal my things and I'd shout and slam doors and complain (sorry about that – but at least you can probably relate a little bit now). But I'd still take you to the park and glow with pride at your improvement on drawings and tell everyone about my little sister's funny antics.

It was weird when you started going to school, and you'd come home with phrases and lessons you'd learned about things that I didn't teach you. I couldn't help but feel the slightest bit jealous when you started talking about your new friends and teachers; you were mine! You found me, only me, fascinating and I was your only friend, but I thankfully grew out of that as I grew out of the extreme insecurity that teenagehood brings.

This is probably where your own memory starts to creep in, and I can talk about the moments we both remember: like you hiding in my cupboard when trying to film 'Stuck The Way We Are' (for my readers, this is a duet I wrote about our age gap when Hedy was seven and I was seventeen), or us playing with Lego on the landing and giggling like monkeys in the corner of rooms at family events. We would run to the park at the bottom of the road and take turns on the swings until the setting sun made us shiver and Mum appeared by the gates to shout at us to come back for dinner. We adored each other and, despite the age gap and the occasional bickering, we were best friends in the most special way.

* * *

Little nauseous Dodie could never have fathomed the impact you have had on my life.

(We're going to get slightly dramatic here, but if there was a chapter that had to have it this one would be the one that deserves it the most.)

When I say that I'm proud of you, no one will ever understand the magnitude of that statement. I am not just proud. I am constantly overwhelmed by your talent, your confidence and your intelligence. You are already a thousand times more objective and kind than I was at your

by Hedy

age, and I just want to show the world how incredible you are, and how much more incredible you will be.

When I say that you inspire me, I mean that you remind me of who I am and why I am alive. You pull me up and bring me pure, real joy when I haven't been able to find it for a while.

And when I say that I love you, words seems pathetically incapable of describing what this means. You are the most important human in the universe, and I would go through absolutely anything just for you to be happy. I have never experienced the amount of care for anyone else as I have with you, and I am so lucky to know this feeling because it is so intense, it must be so rare.

I'm excited for all the years we have to mime our favourite musicals to each other, to have sleepovers and gossip about our emotions before we fall asleep, and to grow up and experience life as sisters together. You have already taught me so much, but you are going to grow so much more in the years to come, and I can't wait for you to become even cooler a person than you already are. It is so funny to me that I couldn't understand how I would love you; and it must have been because it was so much more than anything I could have ever dreamed of experiencing.

You'll either be cringing or crying at all of this. Probably both.

ANYWAY. I love you. Thank you for everything. If I'm ever a crappy sister, you have permission to force me to sit and listen to you rap the entirety of Hamilton until you are content.

Love Dodie x

LITTLE ROOM

Goodbye, little room, you've served me well,
I'm sorry for all the nail polish and tea I've spilled.
You saw my secrets, my fears, my best friend, my tears,
my loved and lost encased inside these walls.
A little girl grew up in here,
she's far too grown up to live here any more.

If I'm honest, the bunk bed won hands down.
I almost miss the fuchsia floor and dressing gown,
flower stickers, books and toys, cringey notes to year six boys,
now a tenancy agreement's on the floor.
A little girl grew up in here,
she's far too grown up to live here any more.

So here we are, the final goodbye,
I've got to leave the nest but I'm not sure how to fly.
Thank you, room, you'll always be my warmest place, a home to me.
Turn off the lights and finally close the door.
A little girl grew up in here,
she's far too grown up to live here any more.

A BROKEN FAMILY

Once upon a time, there was a family of five. They all lived in a dusty, dark house with four bedrooms, crammed with thousands of forgotten objects like old books, broken paddling pools, baskets of school reports and photographs, argument-inducing board games and boxes of tools and other DIY supplies.

There was a mum, and she was happiest matching her daughter in a fluffy dressing gown with a glass of wine, dishes cleaned, and Saturday night TV playing in front of her. She'd pick up her children from school and joyfully listen to them babbling about their days, pouring them glasses of orange juice and writing them notes for their lunchboxes for the next day.

There was a dad, and he was happiest lying back on the sofa with his family, watching a loud movie in the summer with the curtains shut to block out the sunshine. Afterwards, he'd open the curtains and the orange glow of the setting sun would tempt him and his children outside. He'd watch them have space hopper races and practise their cartwheels, and after a cigarette or two he'd join in, flipping frisbees and jogging across the garden, laughing loudly.

There were three children. One was a boy, who was growing into a man. He enjoyed the comfort of his bedroom, but would occasionally emerge and interact, winding up his sisters and chasing them up the stairs, loud stomps and giggles booming through the house. The other two were girls: one a child, one a teen. They both danced around their rooms and dreamed of bigger, colourful worlds, holding hands and harmonising in the echo-y bathroom, drawing flowers in the wet fog on the mirror.

The house was never fully clean since it was jam packed with so much stuff, so the mum would clean around it, every day; flustering and dusting over piles and piles of DVDs, hoovering stained carpets and scooping out loads to wash from the laundry basket that would never be empty. She rushed around, confused as to why she never felt truly fulfilled when her days were full of tasks. She longed for a bright, clean house, in hopes that it would brighten up her soul too, and though she dreamed of a different world it felt impossible to leave the dark life she'd always lived.

Every year or so, the dad would knock down walls and plaster over bricks, sandpapering and sawing for a few weeks. He'd set out for change and start – but would come across a problem every time that would drain the spark of determination he'd somehow found. These rooms would then remain with concrete walls and unstable floor boards – unfinished, inconvenient promises that over time would have life scattered and built back on them.

The laughter in the house was matched with shouting on most days, and the kids would often lie in their bedrooms, colouring to the soundtrack of anger and door slamming. Their hearts would sink but they'd still peek through the cracks of their doors, catching each other's eyes and miming along to the yelling, stifling their laughter with sniggers.

Time went by, and the young man packed up a large suitcase and awkwardly hugged everyone goodbye, the three girls crying with their shared sentimental hearts. They walked around and explored their new atmosphere, wondering how things would run with a missing piece. The dad came home in the evenings most nights, and they watched TV together on the sofa, spreading out a little more than usual.

Then the young woman was given something to look after. It was something that she knew couldn't be kept in her home, so she took down some Blu-tacked photos from her wall and packed her little room into a few boxes. Again, the girls sobbed, but unlike the boy she had promised to return, so it didn't hurt too much. She dipped in and out of the family, hopping between her new and old world, making her head spin. The house started to seem darker, and dustier.

The cogs of the family started to change shape through their turning. They all battled on, spinning unhealthily and knocking against each other, denting and damaging one another. Years passed, and the memories of running around together in golden sunlight and sharing a home together seemed more and more distant.

Until one day, the young woman decided to give back what she was given, and the family machine malfunctioned.

There was a year of pain and confusion. No one really knew what to do, and everyone was a little lost. The house, having once been full of shouts and laughter, was quiet.

One by one, they started working on emptying the house. The mum spent her days packing her car with the books and the board games, and bringing them to people who would use them. The children filled bin bags with the broken paddling pools and yellowing school reports. The dad packed up his tools and DIY supplies and lugged them across London to a new flat.

The two girls held hands and harmonised in their old home, the melodies echoing around an empty, dark, dusty house.

The youngest girl and the mum now live in a bright, clean little house, with yellow dining chairs and white tables. The mum cooks for two in the evening and then continues her writing in her fresh, neat bedroom. She listens to the rain on the roof and smiles, while the young girl lies in her bedroom and draws to her favourite music. Every now and again, the dad, son and older girl cram into the little bright house too. It is completely different and utterly the same at once; but it is certainly better, and neither dark nor dusty.

HOMEMADE FAMILY

My brain is working.

Pleasant thoughts are skimming along the surface of my brain, washing over the tissue and coating it in a thin warm layer of milk.

I still can't see, of course. It's too dark, or too light. And I'm a little disappointed, but my heart is held firmly in my chest tonight by strings of friendship. So, although it tugs a little, it can't sink.

One of my friends sniffs, and my subconscious tells me it is my dad. I fade back in and happily internally chuckle at my silly mind.

I look up and lovingly gaze at my homemade family. Laughter bubbles up so easily around these souls and it spills into the room and seals the cracks in the windows and under the door.

Relationships of any kind go through a sort of honeymoon period, of excitement and infatuation, where you feast on the highs of company and saturated experiences. Then comes the anger and irritation, and the future splits into what was, and the rich room I'm in now. Where the mannerisms, predictable jokes and familiarity isn't boring or frustrating, but safe and encompassing and warm.

BEST FRIEND LOVE

* You find something in a shop you know they'd love and crave to buy it to see them happy

* You look for their name in 'attending' lists on Facebook events

* You feel 100% comfortable and calm around them. There is no stress or worry about what to say or how to act

* You value their opinion so highly. Theirs is the most important so you go to them for any advice

* You can message each other saying 'I love you so much by the way' when you become overwhelmed by the thought and not worry about feeling clingy or unbalanced

* You imagine laughing in old age about the arguments you once had, or comparing your wrinkles

* You have at least five private jokes that are guaranteed to crack you up in inappropriate public situations

* * *

Dear best friends,

If I ever forget what I'm doing here, I just have to look to you. Thank you for the dumb jokes, the encouraging paragraph texts, and the shoulders you've let me lay my sad snot on. Thank you for putting up with my temper, my mistakes and occasional carelessness, and my radio silence as replies to your texted questions. I don't appreciate you all anywhere nearly enough; you all inspire me in different ways, and the things I love about myself absolutely came from you. I promise to listen or to talk whenever you need me to, and I promise to work harder at showing you all just how grateful I am for your existence.

xx

I feel like a six out of ten,
I gotta get up early tomorrow again.

What goes on behind the words?
Is there pity for the plain girl?

Can you see the panic inside?
I'm making you uneasy, aren't I?

What goes on behind the words?
Is there pity for the plain girl?
I'll close my mouth, I won't say a word,
a nod of pity for the plain girl.

I know that you don't want me here,
oh, I'll just call a taxi, I gotta be up early tomorrow again.

What goes on behind the words?
Is there pity for the plain girl?
I'll close my mouth, I won't say a word,
a nod of pity for the plain girl.

BULLYING

Like most people, when I was younger, I was bullied. Kids are just mean; but also, I hadn't yet learned that the way to make friends was just to be kind, not to try and make people feel sorry for you by telling stories and lies and constantly seeking sympathy and attention, and that that actually made people feel annoyed and irritated with you. So all through primary school I had people laughing at my shoes and chanting mean nicknames at me in the playground. I'd watch them crowd and whisper to each other, looking at me up and down and then laughing to the group. What I lacked in social awareness I made up for in academics though, and I was in the top set for most of my classes, which, funnily enough, didn't help the teasing. I was called a boffin, teacher's pet, and everyone called me dodecahedron (which looking back is honestly hilarious). My parents and other family members told me everyone was just jealous, and that they were probably bullied too, but of course that made no sense to me. So I downplayed my slightly more pronounced English accent, swore when the other kids dared me to, and screamed at my mum when she forced me to wear a bulky coat and waterproof shoes to school.

When I was in secondary school, or high school, the names got slightly more creative and I sank lower in the hierarchy of popularity. There was a girl on our bus who carried a rainbow bag and didn't care too much about washing her hair, and she liked to tell stories about being magical. So I called her a witch, and the people who'd punch the back of my chair and stuff crisp packets into my pencil case told me I was a legend, and laughed with me, at her. The next week someone sitting behind me would pull my hair and I'd hear them sniggering my colourful nickname, but now and again I'd be on their side, and the hot, sinking guilt of watching that girl fight tears as we laughed at her seemed to be worth the relief of fake acceptance.

I grew up and learned some lessons, as did all of my classmates, and the name calling and shaming faded into indifference. I had a wonderful group of friends, but the bullying from my previous years left me feeling insecure and terrified around strangers. I'd sit back in a conversation, possible sentences flashing in my head, but then just sitting there as I lacked the confidence to throw them out in a space between the chatter. If I managed to collect enough courage to let my ideas escape, the adrenaline in my body would make them come out mumbled and stuttered, and they would flop. People would talk over me and I'd vow to just never try again.

Making videos helped enormously. I could practise my quirks alone, and edit out my flops. I'd watch back a well-spoken, witty girl who spoke without pauses or failed jokes. I'd watch other people's slick vlogs and take note of their mannerisms I enjoyed, until I secretly became a collage of my favourite parts of other people. (I felt guilty about that for a while until I realised that everyone is just a collage of their favourite parts of other people.)

My insecurities from bullying thankfully don't affect my conversation any more. They still shine through in my continual second guessing and desperate need to convince everyone that I am likeable! But that is a battle everyone will fight at some point in their lives. To many people, I am likeable; and to some, I might not be.

But that's okay.

* * *

To the girl with the rainbow bag

You are loveable. You are confident, you are bright, and you are brave. You aren't afraid to openly love the things that make you happy, and I am so sorry for the unjust treatment you get from that. You do not deserve to be made to feel you are lesser than anyone, especially those who are so mean to you. The things I and everyone else was going through do not excuse the way we treated you, but I hope it'll help you understand that it was never because you did anything wrong. I wish I had been as strong as you are.

SOCIAL DANCE

There are some who don't even need to try,
born with a warm heart, a twinkle in their eye.
Glitter in their words, perfume in their breath,
souls of sunshine and lilac pastel skies.

You will find no such shimmering in here,
oh, there's a wish for some that's shovelled down by fear.
Am I happy or just hopeful?
Confident or boastful?
Do people smile holding back a sneer?

Sometimes I wish that I could be
a kinder, better me, for all.
Sometimes I wish that I could be
someone who isn't me, at all.

So off you go, perform your social dance,
outstretched opinions, and a flexible stance.
Pirouette for show, but never let them know
that really you're just begging for a chance.

Sometimes I wish that I could be
A kinder, better me, for all.
Sometimes I wish that I could be
someone who isn't me, at all.

Can someone please tell me how it feels
to say the perfect words, a model of appeal.
Should I spill secrets inside, or should I just hide?
I'll never be okay to reveal.

Sometimes I wish that I could be
a kinder, better me, for all.
Sometimes I wish that I could be
someone who isn't me, at all.

PAIN

I'm currently lying pretty much spread-eagled on a cushioned table with a paper towel underneath my bare bum. I'm trying to distract myself from the pain of this woman rubbing hot wax on my . . . areas . . . and ripping out hundreds of hairs from their little homes in my skin, so I thought I'd write about it. Holy heck, OW.

If anyone asks, I'm not good with pain. I'm actually pretty sure I'm better than most people, but what I'm terrible at is the anxiety. The pre-worry is always SO much worse than the actual act, so I tell people I'm bad so that they'll take extra care of me. I want to know what's happening, when, and how bad it will be, so I can worry/prepare enough for it.

Oh, holy MOLY, my poor little legs. I don't dare look down for fear that she's actually ripping off my skin.

This goes for all kinds of pain. Whether that's ripping hair follicles out (the current situation), tattoos, operations, or heartbreak. Give me a scale of 1–10 and I'll prepare for three times that. It's almost definitely a coping mechanism from my brain. If I anticipate the absolute worse then when the pain does come, it won't feel so bad compared to what I imagined it to be, right?

I guess it helps, in a way. I'm always much more okay than I think I'll be. As I said, the problem lies within the obsessing around the pain. My brain goes haywire and imagines all sorts of horrible tortuous scenarios where I end up going fully mad due to unbearable, uncontrollable pain. Mmmmm. Lovely.

YIKES BIKINI LINE. OW OW OW.

Anyway, I don't think the answer is to tell myself it won't be as bad as I think. Like I said, it's almost handy to anticipate the absolute worst so it's never as bad, so I wouldn't want to lose that. What I absolutely do need to work on is accepting the time for what it is, moment by moment. Half an hour ago I was shivering in a waiting room with sweaty palms and pits, head spinning, chest contracted. Which is all very silly, because the worst thing that was happening to me at that particular moment in time was that the chair was a bit cold on my bare legs, and that doesn't really warrant that sort of bodily response now, does it?

I'm being asked to spread my butt cheeks apart. I'll wrap this up.

Ultimately, you will be okay, and you can learn from your pain. Use it for #art. Also, try looking at it from a different angle – sometimes you can choose to laugh through it. Create your own anaesthetic to tint your memory with brightness, and you will come out stronger, smarter and smoother. Or maybe that's just when you're getting waxed.

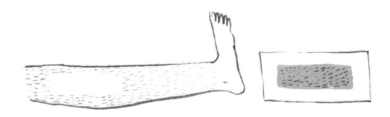

BECOMING WOMAN

Here's something I've learned. If there are quite a lot of people raving on about something, their point is probably valid, and you should probably listen and believe them.

I really wanted to side with the men when I was a little girl. What were all these angry feminists doing? Calm your shit, ladies. You're creating a hate cycle – you get angry, men start hating you, you get angry at mean men. Isn't it obvious? Just be chill; if you're on their side then they'll be nice to you.

(. . . what a fucked up way to live.)

I'd grown up with men in white vans honking their horns and shouting pet names out their window while me and my friends walked back from the bus stop. I was taught (by men) that my worth was in my looks, my sex – and so, though it made me uncomfortable as a fourteen-year-old to know that these older men were looking at my thighs, I again tried to side with the winning team and 'take it as a compliment'.

I stopped being a little girl, but I noticed that I didn't stop being treated as one. Men enjoyed leaning and talking over me in meetings, or spewing out information about topics I wasn't interested in and didn't care to know much about. I felt stupid because I was being made to feel stupid. I think the worst part is that no man really does it on purpose – it's a subconscious, engrained tactic to assert their dominance and power.

I couldn't count for you the amount of times I've had unwanted sexual contact and felt the overwhelming reaction of guilt and shame.

Once it was on a train. It was crowded and bumpy, and a hand kept reaching up my skirt and stroking my knickers. Every time it stopped I wondered if I was dreaming, but whenever it was happening it was so real, and horrible. I wasn't sure if it warranted a scene, and I was with my little sister and my mum so I didn't want to make them upset. I felt sick, panicked and dirty, and I blinked back tears and forced a smile.

Another was by a friend. He asked for hugs all the time and I gave them when he pouted. We shared a bed on a holiday with another friend but this boy insisted on sleeping next to me. I lay like a rock, my stomach sinking with discomfort, while his hands rubbed up my legs and the lower parts of my tummy. I buckled up the courage to whisper a 'stop' in the silence, and he retreated and rolled over. I immediately felt guilty, but five minutes later his hands were back. I stared into the face of my other friend who was sleeping, begging for him to wake up and save me because I couldn't figure out how else to end this.

Mostly it was by my ex-boyfriend, the man I was in love with for two years. He'd grab my hands and place them where he wanted. I'd pull them away and try to laugh it off, but he'd frown and turn cold, asking me why I didn't love him any more. My hips were grabbed and I was pulled on top; I'd shake my head and try to find a way to say no without making him angry. But everything he was saying made sense. What kind of a woman was I if I didn't want to please my man?

* * *

As women, we have fought for our right to vote, to work. We can become astronauts, doctors, filmmakers, wrestlers, whatever. But it's harder to do that in a world that favours men, and especially when we're all damaged from the trauma that being female will bring. I grew up in a world where mothers told me to 'watch out for men trying to get into your pants'. I was advised to pack a pair of flats if I was walking home from a party so I could run away. My friend carried a rape alarm from the age of fourteen. If you're female, these tactics will not be unfamiliar to you.

And yet, despite all of us experiencing constant patronising, sexism and abuse, I am so proud to be a woman, because we are so strong. We push onwards, and we fight with love and empathy.

I feel so sorry for the little girl who felt that the only way to survive was to shut up and suffer.

GRIEF

I saw my dead grandpa lying in a coffin when I was seven years old. His skin was pink, plump and cold, and I cried because I was supposed to and because everyone was so sad.

My cat died when I was ten. We wrapped his little body up in a blue towel and buried him in the garden. I sobbed heavily when I woke up every morning for about two weeks.

My granny started to get ill when I was beginning my GCSE year.

Thursday 23 February
2012

Well,

That's it.

Granny passed away today, at
9:20am. I was told about an
hour ago.

It really hasn't sunk in. I don't know
I just don't know.

I don't want to think about her
warming my hands, or cherry drops,
or that the sun had his hat on today.
I don't want to mum. It's too
painful.

When mum told me actually,
she didn't really. She was crying,
but I didn't know. I just thought
Granny had gotten worse or
something

But how much more worse
could she get?

Sobbing into mum's shoulder,
I said   "is she...?"

I felt mum nod.

Haven't told anyone yet.

She had told me that one day she would be gone, but she would point to the sky and say that she would always be there, with God, looking down on us. I prayed to this God every night, begging him for more time. 'Please at least let her see Hedy turn five years old,' I'd whisper in bed. 'I'm not ready. I'm not strong enough.'

At the end of each hospital visit I would squeeze her hands softly and tell her I loved her. As we walked out of the ward I would stare back until we turned the corner, desperate to hold on to the sight of her for as long as possible, just in case it was the last time I would see her. This was our routine for the next two years, but exam time got heavier, and visits and late night bargaining with God became less frequent.

I bounded out of school with my friend Neb. We had recently become closer; he had lost his dad a few years before, and it was helpful to talk to someone who knew about the hospital visits and the terrible atmosphere at home. From the gates I recognised my mum's car, and I was happily surprised at the idea that I would be given a lift home instead of having to get the bus. I skipped towards the window and knocked. My mum sat, hunched, staring into nothing.

Neb's hand appeared on my shoulder. 'I'll see you tomorrow. Call me later,' he said and squeezed, and hurried ahead. He definitely knew before I did.

My face fell.

I got into the car, my head spinning.

She had got worse, I guessed.

Mum just shook her head.

'No,' I yelped. I wasn't ready. I wasn't strong enough.

But this was it. We clung to each other and cried loudly as I tried to take on the weight of reality in my brain. There was so much guilt, regret and anger. My last visit had been two weeks ago. Why hadn't I been in for so long? Did I tell her all the things I wanted her to know? Why didn't I say goodbye?

We drove home, and I shouted at God in my head. 'Why would you do this? I hate you. I begged you for it to be okay and you gave me nothing.'

* * *

My friend Josh hadn't come into sixth form for the last few weeks. He and I were two of four students from our A level music class, and we'd all banter with Mr Butler, playing 'Für Elise' on the crappy school keyboards and moaning over the time signatures of our set works. He would show me the shapes of chords and then pass me the guitar, helping to hold my fingers down on the frets to limit the buzzing while I strummed. He would let me quickly scribble down his notes from the homework I didn't do while keeping a lookout for sir to come into class. He would take the chair with a crack down the middle that pinched legs if you leaned a certain way so that us other three would be comfortable. But that chair had remained empty for a while, and we all frowned and shrugged at each other when we'd walk in and he wouldn't be there.

We heard the word everyone dreads to hear, but immediately with a 'don't worry'. Apparently it had been caught early, and there was a high chance of a full recovery from this type of cancer.

I started to talk to God again.

Six months later he came into school in non-uniform and with a bald head, but we didn't talk about it. I sat on the cracked chair and we played guitar, filling him in on what he'd missed.

Two weeks later me and my friend sobbed into each other's shoulders in the girls' loos by the vending machines. I thought about shouting at God again, but it felt like no one had ever heard me at all.

* * *

We have all heard of the stages of grief, but I had never realised just how prominent the 'anger' part of it would be. Loss just didn't make sense! There was no good out of it! There was no reason, there were no new chapters; it just fucking sucked and that was it. The world had lost good people, and had damaged the good people who were still in it. So the confusion manifested into anger, and I became furious at religion for glorifying something so unfair and painful.

I don't know anything about the universe. I don't know if there was someone or something listening to my begging and screams, and I don't feel like Granny and Josh are watching me type this from comfy clouds. But I know that all things in the universe come to an end, and because we cannot predict or choose when that will be, we have to make the best out of it all. There is no point in fear, guilt or anger. Destiny simply doesn't care, and what will be, will be. Forgive yourself for the goodbye you didn't get to give; remind the people you love how wonderful they are to you. Death is horrible enough, so deal with it with kindness.

FEELING SO MUCH

Someone is potentially angry with me, and my whole world crashes. I'm the worst person in the world. Everything I have become is unbearable. I am awful and I must change.

I like someone; I'm obsessed with them. They must adore me the way I adore them – we will be best friends. This is the start of something ginormous and I'll look back on this first revelation and we'll laugh at our journey.

Someone gives me advice or shares an idea; I research it to shit and decide this will be the thing that changes me. I say goodbye to something in my life and mark it as a giant chapter, a pillar of experience, and I mourn as if a part of me has died. Maybe I just start waking up an hour earlier and I start dreaming of my new life as an early bird; someone who wakes up to watch the sunrise and goes swimming as a way to introduce the day. Today I watered flowers and was convinced this was a turning point in my life. I dreamed of the changes being a morning gardener would bring, and how I'd tell struggling people of the way that filling up a watering can as part of a routine saved my brain.

I've been called dramatic. 'Why does every little thing she goes through have to be some monstrous event?! She's so pretentious. Chill out.'

Yeah, it's exhausting. I have the highest of highs and the lowest of lows, crashing in moments of despair and agony and then soaring up to incredible, epiphanic peaks of life where, suddenly, all the pain and hardship make sense and look just as beautiful as all the good times. Sometimes it's unbearable; and yet I watch people do things like make sensible decisions, walking away from bad relationships because 'in the long run, it'll be better', while I continue to damage myself and write about it, oddly addicted to the excitement of intensified emotions, be they happy or sad.

So, though I don't choose to feel so much all the time, and though it can be ridiculous and incredibly painful – I'm proud of it. I'm excited, I'm reckless, I'm terrified, and because I can hurt so much, I can love so deeply.

MY GRANNY

My granny was the sort of person who would always, always put other people before herself. If you were sick and there was one bed in the room, she'd insist on sleeping on the hard floor beside you in case you needed help in the night. She would be up early in the morning to make you sweet tea and bread fried in butter with peppery eggs, making far too much, and then offering you cake or biscuits, giggling and pushing it towards you when you laid your hands on your plump tummy and shook your head. If you wanted to paint pictures and play arts and crafts, she'd lay out a tablecloth, bring you the pots, and then wash all the brushes and wipe away the smears on the floor once you were bored and had ran away; until you'd totter back, asking to paint again and without a word or tut she'd lay it all out again, cooing with encouragement at your rainbow splotches.

Granny was kind, but she was in no way weak. Her compassion was her principle, and she stuck by that no matter what. She would not tolerate shouting or telling off, and she would watch Dad get angry at our messy rooms stone-faced, fuming internally at the way he could bellow. As children, me and Iain enjoyed being tickled, but this was something else she was against; she would hear our squeals and panic, squeaking at us to stop as it was bad for 'the nerves'.

Granny would talk a lot about 'the nerves'. When I had my stomach migraines she would sit on my duvet, stroking my head and holding my hand to try to stop the nerves from hurting me. She would buy us magazines and toys and tell us to stop doing homework, because it was too much for the nerves. I feel like Granny felt the nerves a lot, and she mustn't have wanted us to feel them either.

Right until the end, Granny stuck to her principles of goodness as best she could for someone who was losing herself slowly. She would bat the nurses away who would fuss over her, and insist on getting out of her hospital bed to hobble to the loos by herself. And once her brain didn't let her recognise us when we walked in the ward with broken hearts, carrying flowers, she somehow knew it was time to go.

My granny taught me the importance of true selflessness, and the strength of moral standards. I am proud to carry her empathy and giving nature, and I know I will pass down that part of her to my children, and their children too.

Encore

I WON'T BE DONE

I won't be done,
I think my head is fit to burst;
which breakdown shall I deal with first?
I have to close my eyes
to keep my thoughts inside.

How many palpitations can you take on?
Ten confrontations and I'm still standing strong!
I may not like my thighs,
but at least my body keeps me alive.

So let's breathe one, two, three, four,
till the world gives you some more.

Do you think
it'll ever stop?
Will I miss this
when it's all gone?

Watch me beg
for some peace!
And when it comes –
I won't be done.

How did I get on this path?
Time and fate are trying to make me laugh.
A woman with a teenage brain
attempts to play the grown-up game.

So let's breathe one, two, three, four,
till the world gives you some more.

Do you think
it'll ever stop?
Will I miss this
when it's all gone?

Watch me beg
for some peace!
And when it comes –
I won't be done.

We can take it!
We might break, but
I've broken before, and I will break again,
so give me some more –
I'll be here till the end.

Yeah, we will lose it,
you know we'll use it!
I've broken before, and I will break again,
so give me some more –
I'll be here till the end.

HOPES FOR THE FUTURE

I will always grow. I will hurt and change and I'll get better at knowing when it is time to be sad and when it is time to try to be happy. I will learn how to find love for myself by myself, and not to look for it from people who give it out rarely as a way to convince myself I am special enough. Younger Dodies will sit in my head and come out when I need them: seven-year-old me will burst out whenever there's a swimming pool or a playground nearby; fifteen-year-old me might take a little look around when I've forgotten how to talk to people who recognise me online; eighteen-year-old me will remind me that I am never alone, and my wonderful friends will always be around to make me feel better. And twenty-two-year-old me will stand strong against madness, proof that pain can be used to learn, and to create wonderful things.

ACKNOWLEDGEMENTS

Thank you to my English teachers in school – Mrs Phillips, Ms Truman, Mrs Tedman and Mrs Croft – for showing me how writers craft hidden stories and messages into their words, and inspiring me to do just that. To Jaqueline Wilson for the worlds I grew up reading about and have carried around with me.

Thanks Josh and Richard for making all this happen. To the Ebury team (Sara, Michelle, Clarissa and Kealey) for their support, understanding and encouragement; Ben for his wonderful illustrations; and Dave for using the aesthetic eye that I lack and designing something beautiful.

Thank you to the people who have listened to my music, watched my videos, read my Instagram posts; there will never be a kinder, cooler community to be in.

Thank you to my family for encouraging my creative endeavours; thank you to my friends for helping me through my madness; and thank you to my brain for somehow managing to finish writing a book in a depressive state.